Math for College and Career Readiness

Grade 6

Authors:	Christine Henderson (Ed.), Karise Mace, Stephen Fowler, Amy Jones-Lewis
Editor:	Mary Dieterich
Proofreaders:	April Albert and Margaret Brown

COPYRIGHT © 2016 Mark Twain Media, Inc.

ISBN 978-1-62223-583-4

Printing No. CD-404238

Mark Twain Media, Inc., Publishers
Distributed by Carson-Dellosa Publishing LLC

Visit us at www.carsondellosa.com

Table of Contents

Introduction to the Teacher

Up to half of students entering college elect "undecided" for their major, and an estimated three out of four students change their majors at least once before graduation. This is, in part, due to the fact that middle- and high-school students do not have much exposure to the variety of careers available to today's work force. This workbook is designed to give middle-school students an idea of existing careers and the background and skills necessary to be successful in those careers.

The first three units focus on jobs students could do right now to start building their resumes and earning some money. The next three units focus on careers that require at least some post-secondary schooling. The final three units emphasize STEM-related careers, where science, technology, engineering, and mathematics play a significant part.

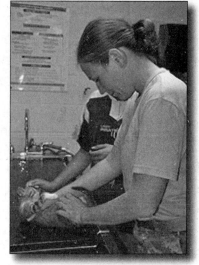

Each unit is aligned to the Common Core State Standards for Mathematics. This correlation is included on the teacher page at the beginning of each unit. The units also support the NCTM standards. The teacher page includes background on the career, the average median salary listed by the 2015 U.S. Bureau of Labor Statistics, a detailed explanation of the topics covered in the unit, and a list of prerequisite skills necessary to complete the unit.

We hope your students enjoy exploring these different careers and that this exploration helps prepare them for college and their future careers.

—Stephen Fowler, Christine Henderson, Amy Jones-Lewis, and Karise Mace

Unit 1: The Mathematics of Lemonade Stands

Introduction

Operating a lemonade stand is a great way to spend time with friends on a nice day while learning about what it takes to run a business. Almost anyone can run a lemonade stand, but running a successful one requires mathematics, such as understanding ratios and proportions, calculating values with rational numbers, solving basic equations, and working with money.

Whether using a powdered mix or making all-natural lemonade from fresh ingredients, ratios and proportions are the fundamental tools used to mix large quantities of lemonade from a basic recipe designed to make only a small amount. Having enough lemonade to sell to a lot of customers is essential to running a successful lemonade stand. Understanding how to adjust the size of a recipe using ratios and proportions is extremely important.

Deciding how many cups of lemonade to pour, figuring out how much to sell to break even, and splitting profits among everyone running the lemonade stand require working with rational numbers and solving equations. These are necessary skills to keep a lemonade stand going.

Whether to raise money for charity or save up to buy a nice gift, the purpose of a lemonade stand is to make money. Every time a cup of lemonade is sold or ingredients to make more lemonade are purchased, calculations involving money are made. As a result, having strong money-related math skills is essential to running a successful lemonade stand.

These are just some of the ways mathematics is used to run a business and will be the focus of this unit as students explore the math needed to operate a lemonade stand.

Common Core State Standards

This unit addresses the following Common Core State Standards:

- CCSS.Math.Content.6.RP.A.2
- CCSS.Math.Content.6.RP.A.3
- CCSS.Math.Content.6.NS.A.1
- CCSS.Math.Content.6.NS.B.3
- CCSS.Math.Content.6.EE.B.6
- CCSS.Math.Content.6.EE.B.7

Prerequisite Skills

Prior to completing this unit, students should be proficient in the following mathematical skills: (Note: A practice sheet has been provided for each skill listed.)

- Solving problems involving ratios and proportions
- Adding, subtracting, multiplying, and dividing rational numbers
- Working with money

Name: _____   Date: _____

Unit 1: The Mathematics of Lemonade Stands

Prerequisite Skill Practice—Ratios and Proportions

Directions: Complete each exercise as indicated. Show your work. The first problem has been worked out as an example.

1. The ratio of girls to boys in a class is 3:1. How many boys are in the class if there are 21 girls in the class? $$\frac{3}{1} = \frac{21}{x}$$ $$x \cdot 3 = 1 \cdot 21$$ $$3x = 21$$ $$x = 21 \div 3$$ $$x = 7 \quad \text{There are 7 boys in the class.}$$	**2.** A recipe calls for $2\frac{1}{4}$ cups of flour and $1\frac{1}{2}$ cups of sugar. How many cups of sugar are needed for 9 cups of flour?
3. Determine the value of n (write your answer as a decimal): $$\frac{n}{32} = \frac{9}{20}$$	**4.** Determine the value of x (write your answer as a mixed number): $$\frac{8}{15} = \frac{x}{40}$$
5. The ratio of cars to trucks on a particular road is 10:3. How many cars are on the road if there are 42 trucks on the road?	**6.** Determine the value of a (write your answer as an improper fraction): $$\frac{6}{a} = \frac{21}{34}$$
7. Determine the value of c: $$\frac{11}{19} = \frac{7}{c}$$	**8.** A word contains 5 consonants for every 3 vowels. How many letters are in the word if it contains 9 vowels?

Name: _____ Date: _____

Unit 1: The Mathematics of Lemonade Stands

Prerequisite Skill Practice—Operations With Rational Numbers

Directions: Calculate each value as indicated. Show your work. Write your answer as a simplified fraction or mixed number. The first problem has been worked out as an example.

1. $17\frac{3}{10} - 8\frac{1}{6}$ $17\frac{3}{10} - 8\frac{1}{6} = 17\frac{9}{30} - 8\frac{5}{30}$ $= 9\frac{4}{30}$ $= 9\frac{2}{15}$	**2.** $7\frac{1}{5} \div 6\frac{3}{4}$
3. $12\frac{3}{4} \cdot 8\frac{1}{2}$	**4.** $9\frac{3}{8} + 2\frac{5}{6}$
5. $12\frac{1}{2} \div 4\frac{1}{6}$	**6.** $\frac{4}{7} \cdot 2\frac{1}{10}$
7. $10\frac{7}{12} + 1\frac{2}{3}$	**8.** $7\frac{3}{4} - 2\frac{5}{6}$
9. $\frac{7}{8} - \frac{7}{9}$	**10.** $4\frac{3}{8} \div \frac{2}{5}$

Name: _____　Date: _____

Unit 1: The Mathematics of Lemonade Stands

Prerequisite Skill Practice—Working With Money

Directions: Complete each exercise as directed. Show your work. Be sure to label your final answers. The first problem has been worked out as an example.

1. What is the total cost of 8 pounds of bananas if bananas cost 49¢ per pound? $8 \cdot 0.49 = 3.92$ The total cost is $3.92.	**2.** Determine the cost of one baseball if a case containing one dozen baseballs costs $45.00.
3. Grace and Henri want to use binders to organize their files. Grace purchases 15 binders to organize her files for a total of $44.25. Henri purchases 25 binders to organize his files. How much did Henri spend on his binders?	**4.** Brandon has $175.00 to spend on new clothes to start the school year. He purchases 2 pairs of jeans for $24.95 each, 3 shirts for $12.50 each, and a pair of shoes for $70.00. How much money does Brandon have left?
5. Juanita and Jorge are paid a total of $2,400 to paint a house. If Juanita earns twice as much as Jorge, how much is Jorge paid?	**6.** What is the total amount paid for a new sofa that costs $899.00 if sales tax is 6%?
7. What is the sale price of an item marked 40% off if the original price was $12.95?	**8.** How many cartridges of printer ink can be purchased with $100.00 if each cartridge costs $16.99?

Name: _____   Date: _____

Unit 1: The Mathematics of Lemonade Stands

Real-World Application

If you like to work with friends or family while meeting new people and making money, operating a lemonade stand might be a great thing to do. As with many adventures in life, running a lemonade stand requires the use of mathematics, and we will explore some of that mathematics in this unit.

The ingredients for a basic lemonade recipe are as follows:

Basic Lemonade Recipe

6 lemons

$\frac{3}{4}$ cup sugar

$1\frac{1}{2}$ quarts water

When determining approximately how much lemonade the recipe makes, you look at only the amount of water used. In this case, the recipe makes approximately $1\frac{1}{2}$ quarts of lemonade.

Directions: Using this recipe as a guide, imagine that you and some friends open a lemonade stand in your neighborhood. Work through the exercises that follow to explore what it takes to succeed.

1. At the local market, lemons are priced 5 for $2.00. What is the unit cost per lemon?

_____

2. A bag containing 9 cups of sugar sells for $2.25. How much does each cup of sugar cost?

_____

Name: _____ Date: _____

Unit 1: The Mathematics of Lemonade Stands

Real-World Application (cont.)

3. You want to make 2 gallons, which is 8 quarts, of lemonade to sell. By what factor do you need to multiply the given recipe in order to make that much lemonade? Write your answer as a mixed number. Explain how you determined your answer.

_____

_____

_____

4. How many lemons and how much sugar do you need in order to make the 2 gallons of lemonade you want to sell? Use mathematics to support your answers.

_____

_____

Name: _____ Date: _____

Unit 1: The Mathematics of Lemonade Stands

Real-World Application (cont.)

5. Use your answers to #1–4 to determine how much you need to spend on lemons and sugar in order to make 2 gallons of lemonade. Explain how you determined your answer.

_____

_____

_____

6. You decide to sell 8-ounce cups of lemonade at your lemonade stand. Given that there are 128 ounces per gallon, how many cups of lemonade do you sell if you go through the entire 2 gallons you make? Use mathematics to support your answer.

_____

_____

_____

Name: _____ Date: _____

Unit 1: The Mathematics of Lemonade Stands

Real-World Application (cont.)

7. You sell each cup of lemonade for $0.75. Use your answer to #6 to determine how much income you earn if you sell the entire 2 gallons of lemonade.

_____

8. You run your lemonade stand both Saturday and Sunday. You make and sell 2 gallons of lemonade each day. Use your answers to #5 and #7 to calculate your profit for the weekend. (Note: profit is the difference between the amount of income you earn and the amount of money you spend.) Use mathematics to support your answer.

_____

_____

_____

Name: _____ Date: _____

Unit 1: The Mathematics of Lemonade Stands

Real-World Application (cont.)

9. Three friends help you run your lemonade stand over the weekend: Alfonso, Bethany, and Charlene. Alfonso helps Saturday, Bethany helps Sunday, and Charlene helps both days. How should you divide the profit calculated in #8 so each of you working the lemonade stand receives a fair share? Explain how you determined your answer and use mathematics to support it.

_____

_____

_____

_____

10. Give two changes you might consider to increase the profit earned from your lemonade stand and explain why those changes would lead to an increased profit for you. Then discuss what problems might arise by making those changes.

_____

_____

_____

_____

_____

_____

_____

Unit 2: The Mathematics of Dog Walking

Introduction

Dog walking is one way that sixth graders can earn money. A good dog walker must love dogs and understand how to work with and manage them. They need to know which dogs work well together and how much exercise each of the dogs need. Some dogs, such as Labrador Retrievers, are full of energy and love to socialize. They quickly make friends with other dogs and need lots of exercise. Other dogs, such as Affenpinschers, are not as friendly with unfamiliar dogs and do not need much exercise. A dog walker must carefully plan their schedule so as not to end up walking incompatible dogs at the same time.

It is also important for a dog walker to have some business sense. Recruiting clients and other dog walkers and managing money and time are important skills. A dog walker must plan how much time to spend on their business each week; that time must be divided between dog walking and administrative tasks, like scheduling and record keeping. A dog walker who knows how to keep good records and analyze them can use that information to help the business grow.

These are just some of the ways mathematics are used to run a business and will be the focus of this unit as students explore the math needed to run a dog-walking business.

Common Core State Standards

This unit addresses the following Common Core State Standards:

- CCSS.Math.Content.6.NS.B.4
- CCSS.Math.Content.6.NS.C.7c
- CCSS.Math.Content.6.EE.A.2a
- CCSS.Math.Content.6.EE.B.6
- CCSS.Math.Content.6.EE.B.8

- CCSS.Math.Content.6.SP.A.2
- CCSS.Math.Content.6.SP.A.3
- CCSS.Math.Content.6.SP.B.4
- CCSS.Math.Content.6.SP.B.5c
- CCSS.Math.Content.6.SP.B.5d

Prerequisite Skills

Prior to completing this unit, students should be proficient in the following mathematical skills: (Note: A practice sheet has been provided for each skill listed.)

- Writing variable expressions and inequalities to represent a situation
- Determining the least common multiple of two or more numbers
- Calculating statistical quantities

Name: _____ Date: _____

Unit 2: The Mathematics of Dog Walking

Prerequisite Skill Practice—Variable Expressions and Inequalities

Directions: Write an expression or inequality to represent the given description. The first problem has been worked out as an example.

1. Joan is five years older than Frederick. Let *f* represent Frederick's age. Write a variable expression that can be used to determine Joan's age. $f + 5$	**2.** Micah creates a playlist with 18 songs on it. Dominique creates a playlist that has *s* fewer songs on it than Micah's playlist. Write a variable expression that can be used to determine the number of songs on Dominque's playlist.
3. Samuel has 23 cousins. Jashanae has *c* more cousins than Samuel. Write an expression that can be used to determine the number of cousins Jashanae has.	**4.** One serving of carrots has *c* calories. One serving of celery has 16 fewer calories than a serving of carrots. Write an expression that can be used to determine the number of calories in a serving of celery.
5. Tamara must earn at least 72 points on her project to get the grade she wants in math. Let *p* represent the number of points Tamara can get on her project. Write an inequality that represents this situation.	**6.** Nicholas has 345 baseball cards. Dillon has fewer baseball cards than Nicholas. Let *d* represent the number of baseball cards Dillon has. Write an inequality that represents this situation.
7. Farmer Brown likes to keep his herd of sheep to 175 or fewer sheep. Let *s* represent the number of sheep Farmer Brown has in his herd. Write an inequality that represents this situation.	**8.** Claudine likes for the balance of her checking account to be more than $500. Let *b* represent the balance of Claudine's checking account. Write an inequality that represents this situation.

Name: _____ Date: _____

Unit 2: The Mathematics of Dog Walking

Prerequisite Skill Practice—Least Common Multiple

Directions: Determine the least common multiple of the given sets of numbers. The first problem has been worked out as an example.

1. 3 and 8 Multiples of 3: 3, 6, 9, 12, 15, 18, 21, 24 Multiples of 8: 8, 16, 24, 32, 40 LCM (3, 8) = 24	**2.** 4 and 9
3. 10 and 12	**4.** 3 and 12
5. 2, 3, and 5	**6.** 4, 6, and 8
7. 2, 5, and 7	**8.** 2, 4, 6, and 9

Name: _____　　Date: _____

Unit 2: The Mathematics of Dog Walking

Prerequisite Skill Practice—Statistical Quantities

Directions: Calculate the mean, mean absolute deviation, and median of each data set. The first problem has been worked out as an example.

---

1. 6, 6, 6, 8, 9, 9, 9, 9, 10

Mean: $\dfrac{6 + 6 + 6 + 8 + 9 + 9 + 9 + 9 + 10}{9} = \dfrac{72}{9} = 8$

MAD: $\dfrac{|6-8| + |6-8| + |6-8| + |8-8| + |9-8| + |9-8| + |9-8| + |9-8| + |10-8|}{9} = \dfrac{12}{9} = 1\dfrac{1}{3}$

Median: 9

---

2. 10, 10, 12, 12, 13, 13, 13, 15, 15, 15, 15

---

3. 22, 23, 26, 28, 33, 36

---

4. 34, 36, 40, 45, 47, 55, 58, 61

Name: _____ Date: _____

Unit 2: The Mathematics of Dog Walking

Real-Life Application

If you love dogs and being outside, then dog walking might be a good job for you. As with most jobs, there is some mathematics involved in being a dog walker, and we will explore some of those mathematic concepts in this unit.

Establishing a Dog-Walking Business

A dog-walking business can be a fun way to earn some money. Although it's hard work, it can be very rewarding. Imagine that you have decided to start a dog-walking business.

1. One of the first decisions you must make is how much time you would like to spend walking dogs each week. List the days and hours that you are willing to commit to your dog-walking business each week.

_____

_____

_____

2. Use your answer to #1 to determine the total number of hours you are willing to commit to your dog-walking business each week.

_____

3. Each week, you will need to spend some time on the administrative part of the job—scheduling, bookkeeping, advertising, etc. Let a represent the amount of time spent on administrative tasks each week. Write an expression that you can use to determine how many hours you will have available for dog walking each week after you complete your administrative tasks.

_____

Name: _____ Date: _____

Unit 2: The Mathematics of Dog Walking

Real-Life Application (cont.)

4. In order to maximize your profits, you will want to minimize the amount of time you spend on administrative tasks so that you can spend most of your time walking dogs. You decide to spend 2 hours or less each week on administrative tasks. Write an inequality that represents the amount of time you can spend each week on administrative tasks.

_____

5. Describe in words the solution set for the inequality that you wrote in #4. Then graph the solution set on the number line below.

_____

_____

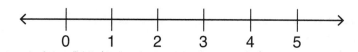

Planning the Walks

6. Imagine that you have six dogs that need to be walked on Wednesday afternoons, but they walk at different paces. As a result, they cannot all be walked together. You have hired two friends, Miranda and D'Shaun, to help you walk these dogs. The table below shows how long it takes each of the dogs to make one loop on the dog path and who their dog walker is.

Name of Dog	Time to Complete One Loop (minutes)	Dog Walker
Mosey	6	You
Sammy	6	You
Leo	8	Miranda
Daisy	8	Miranda
Molly	12	D'Shaun
Henry	12	D'Shaun

Name: _____ Date: _____

Unit 2: The Mathematics of Dog Walking

Real-Life Application (cont.)

a. If you and your friends start walking all of the dogs at the same time, how long will it be before the three of you end up at the starting point at the same time? Explain how you determined your answer and use mathematics to support it.

_____

_____

b. How many loops will each of you have walked with your dogs at that time? Explain how you determined your answer and use mathematics to support it.

_____

_____

7. Several of your clients only need your help walking their dogs every few days. The table below shows how often these dogs need to be walked.

Name of Dog	How frequently you must walk them (days)
Bobo	3
Cleo	2
Izzy	5
Al	6

You walk all four of these dogs on a Monday. How many days will it be until you walk all four dogs on the same day again? Explain how you determined your answer and use mathematics to support it.

_____

_____

Name: _____ Date: _____

Unit 2: The Mathematics of Dog Walking

Real-Life Application (cont.)

Analyzing Your Business

At the end of your first summer as a dog walker, you decide to analyze your business to see if you can make any improvements. The table below shows the data you have collected over the summer.

Week	Time Spent on Administrative Tasks (hours)	Time Spent Walking Dogs (hours)	Number of Dogs Walked
1	3	12	8
2	$1\frac{1}{2}$	14	12
3	$1\frac{3}{4}$	12	9
4	2	16	10
5	$1\frac{1}{2}$	14	12
6	2	14	10
7	1	8	4
8	$1\frac{3}{4}$	16	13

8. Create a dot plot to display the amount of time spent on administrative tasks.

9. What does the dot plot tell you about the amount of time spent on administrative tasks?

_____

_____

_____

_____

Name: _____ Date: _____

Unit 2: The Mathematics of Dog Walking

Real-Life Application (cont.)

10. Create a dot plot to display the amount of time spent walking dogs.

11. What does the dot plot tell you about the amount of time spent walking dogs?

_____

_____

_____

_____

12. Calculate the mean amount of time you spent on administrative tasks per week. Explain what it means in this context.

_____

_____

13. Calculate the mean amount of time you spent walking dogs in a week. Explain what it means in this context.

_____

_____

Name: _____ Date: _____

Unit 2: The Mathematics of Dog Walking

Real-Life Application (cont.)

14. Calculate the mean absolute deviation for the amount of time you spent walking dogs each week. Explain what this means in this context.

_____

_____

15. You interview a friend as a potential dog walker for next summer. She asks how many dogs you walk each week on average.

a. Determine the mean and median number of dogs you walk each week. Show your work.

_____

b. Would you tell your friend the mean or median number of dogs you walk each week? Explain how you determined your answer.

_____

_____

_____

_____

Unit 3: The Mathematics of Fundraisers

Introduction

Nearly every sports team, robotics team, and marching band has one thing in common—fundraising! Selling candy, wrapping paper, t-shirts, pizzas, or cookies is a regular part of participating in these activities. The money raised by these fundraisers goes to purchase much-needed supplies: new uniforms, safety equipment, tools, or instruments. Sometimes the fundraisers pay for the buses used to transport the participants to their competitions throughout the season.

The mathematics of a fundraiser is extensive, but it's focused on one major question: How do we raise the money that we will need to purchase what we need? Organizers of the fundraisers have to consider what they should sell, how much they make on each sale, and how many items they need to sell. If they don't compute correctly, they could end up wasting their time, or worse, losing money.

These are just some of the ways mathematics are used to carry out a fundraiser and will be the focus of this unit as students explore the math needed for a baseball little league to make money from a fundraiser.

Common Core State Standards

This unit addresses the following Common Core State Standards:

- CCSS.Math.Content.6.RP.A.1
- CCSS.Math.Content.6.RP.A.3B
- CCSS.Math.Content.6.NS.B.2
- CCSS.Math.Content.6.NS.B.3
- CCSS.Math.Content.6.EE.B.7

Prerequisite Skills

Prior to completing this unit, students should be proficient in the following mathematical skills: (Note: A practice sheet has been provided for each skill listed.)

- Using ratio language to describe a ratio relationship between two quantities
- Dividing multi-digit numbers using the standard algorithm
- Solving unit rate problems

Name: _____ Date: _____

Unit 3: The Mathematics of Fundraisers

Prerequisite Skill Practice—Writing Ratios

Directions: For each of the following, use ratio language to describe the relationship between two quantities in two different ways. Use complete sentences. The first problem has been worked out as an example.

1. At lunchtime, there were 15 hamburgers and 5 hotdogs ordered. The ratio of hamburgers to hotdogs sold is 15:5. For every hotdog that was sold, 3 hamburgers were sold.	2. Maurice put 9 green apples and 7 red apples in his grocery cart.
3. Sarah owns 8 Wii games and 6 PS3 games.	4. 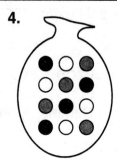
5. In Ms. Holt's classroom, there are 14 girls and 10 boys.	6. At an ice cream shop, 12 vanilla cones and 18 chocolate cones were sold.
7. 	8. The movie theater sold 125 bags of popcorn and 210 boxes of candy on Sunday.

Name: _____ Date: _____

Unit 3: The Mathematics of Fundraisers

Prerequisite Skill Practice—Division With Multi-Digit Numbers

Directions: For each of the following, divide the numbers using the standard algorithm. Show your work. The first problem has been worked out as an example.

1. 13,410 ÷ 47 $$\begin{array}{r} 285 \text{ r } 15 \\ 47\overline{)13410} \\ -\underline{94} \\ 401 \\ -\underline{376} \\ 250 \\ -\underline{235} \\ 15 \end{array}$$	**2.** 2,421 ÷ 5
3. 86,450 ÷ 91	**4.** 9,304 ÷ 19
5. 3,392 ÷ 4	**6.** 3,168 ÷ 11
7. 1,627.2 ÷ 72	**8.** 6,111.6 ÷ 22

Name: _____ Date: _____

Unit 3: The Mathematics of Fundraisers

Prerequisite Skill Practice—Unit Rates

Directions: Solve each problem and show your work. The first problem has been worked out as an example.

1. Mitchell wrote 12 pages in 6 hours. At this rate, how many pages will he have written in 10 hours? $$12 \div 6 = 2$$ Mitchell wrote 2 pages per hour. $$2 \cdot 10 = 20$$ Mitchell will have written 20 pages in 10 hours.	2. Lucy took 9 hours to read a 270-page book. At this rate, how long will it take her to read a 390-page book?
3. Kaniah can type 10 words in 15 seconds. How many words does she type per minute?	4. Nine lemons cost $3.24. What is the cost of one lemon?
5. Mai earns $27 for 4.5 hours of babysitting. How much does she make per hour?	6. Davon hikes 2.25 miles in 30 minutes. If he hikes for 7 hours at the same rate, how far will he have gone?
7. Fifteen gallons of gas cost $37.50. At this rate, how much gas can you get for $60?	8. You ran 6 miles in an hour. At this rate, how long will it take you to run 18 miles?

Name: _____   Date: _____

Unit 3: The Mathematics of Fundraisers

Real-Life Application

Fundraisers are only successful if they do what they were intended to do—make money! In designing a fundraiser, special attention needs to be paid to the items that are being sold and the amount of money that can be made from selling them. If no one wants the items or they are too expensive to buy, the fundraiser won't earn enough money to support the project or buy the supplies that are needed. We will explore the mathematics of a successful fundraiser in this unit.

Determining Need

The sixth grade baseball team is raising money to purchase new uniforms and equipment. Mr. Peton, the baseball coach, is organizing the fundraiser with assistance from the team. To begin, Mr. Peton needs to determine how much money the team needs to raise.

1. The uniforms cost $39.89, and the hats cost $9.49. If there are 18 members of the team, how much will the uniforms and the hats cost? Show your work.

_____

2. Catcher's gear costs $349.20, and bats cost $65.49 each. If they need 1 set of catcher's gear and 4 new bats, how much do they need for equipment?

_____

3. Use your answers to #1 and #2 to determine how much money the team needs to raise in all.

_____

Name: _____ Date: _____

Unit 3: The Mathematics of Fundraisers

Real-Life Application (cont.)

Deciding What to Sell

Next, Mr. Peton has to decide which items to sell. He asks the team to survey the students at school.

4. The team wants to sell either t-shirts or sweatshirts. They survey the middle school students at lunch, and 210 students voted for sweatshirts while 126 students voted for t-shirts. Three different team members summarized the results for Mr. Peton. For each comparison, determine if the student wrote a ratio that correctly represents the results. Explain your reasoning.

a. The ratio of students who want sweatshirts compared to t-shirts is 5:3 because for every 5 students who wanted sweatshirts, 3 students wanted t-shirts.

_____

_____

b. There were 84 more student votes for sweatshirts than for t-shirts.

_____

_____

c. Five out of every eight students voted for sweatshirts.

_____

_____

Name: _____   Date: _____

Unit 3: The Mathematics of Fundraisers

Real-Life Application (cont.)

5. The team also wants to sell a food item. They survey the middle school students at lunch and get the following results.

Frozen Pizzas	Cookie Dough
84	252

Summarize the results for Mr. Peton by writing the ratio three different ways. Use complete sentences and ratio language.

_____

_____

_____

    The team decides to sell sweatshirts and cookie dough. Next, they need to consider how much money they can earn from selling these items.

6. If they earn $12 on each sweatshirt, how many sweatshirts do they need to sell to earn at least $1,000 from the sweatshirt sale? Write and solve an inequality to answer the question.

_____

7. If they earn $4.50 on each tub of cookie dough, how many tubs of cookie dough do they need to sell to earn at least $500 from the cookie dough sale? Write and solve an inequality to answer the question.

_____

Name: _____ Date: _____

Unit 3: The Mathematics of Fundraisers

Real-Life Application (cont.)

Now that the team knows how much they need to sell, they get to work making sales.

8. Pedro asks 7 people to buy cookie dough, and 4 people agree to buy a tub. If he continues to sell cookie dough at the same rate, how many people does he need to ask to buy cookie dough in order to meet his personal goal of 16 tubs? Show your work.

_____

9. Dan thinks that he can sell sweatshirts to 3 out of every 4 people that he asks. If he is correct, how many people does he need to ask to meet his personal goal of selling 9 sweatshirts? Show your work.

_____

Name: _____ Date: _____

Unit 3: The Mathematics of Fundraisers

Real-Life Application (cont.)

Checking the Results

The sale is over! Now the team needs to determine if they met their goals.

10. Here are the results. Did the team meet their fundraising goals? Explain how you determined your answer and use mathematics to support it.

Player	Number of Cookie Dough Tubs Sold	Number of Sweatshirts Sold
Nigel	5	4
Colton	6	7
Devan	3	4
Symeon	6	3
Pedro	7	12
Micah	6	6
Xander	12	13
Jack	3	7
Randell	5	2
D'Andre	8	10
Dan	9	4
Ira	6	6
Jayce	6	9
Nikolas	9	5
Slade	2	8
Philip	5	3
Jerry	2	8
Trayvon	7	4

_____

_____

_____

Unit 4: The Mathematics of Educators

Introduction

There are many types of educators in our communities. An educator may be a teacher, administrator, professor, researcher, or publisher. It is important for all educators to be able to compute accurately, represent relationships algebraically, calculate area and volume, and process and evaluate statistical data—even if they are not mathematics teachers.

The median annual wage for teachers is $54,000. Teachers in all disciplines and grade levels regularly calculate student grades to determine whether or not they are mastering the course content. They organize their classrooms and supplies and evaluate statistical data about their students so that they can better serve their educational needs.

These are just some of the ways mathematics is used by educators and will be the focus of this unit as students explore the math that teachers use to make decisions.

Common Core State Standards

This unit addresses the following Common Core State Standards:

- CCSS.Math.Content.6.NS.B.3
- CCSS.Math.Content.6.NS.C.6b
- CCSS.Math.Content.6.NS.C.6c
- CCSS.Math.Content.6.NS.C.8
- CCSS.Math.Content.6.EE.A.2a

- CCSS.Math.Content.6.EE.A.2c
- CCSS.Math.Content.6.EE.B.7
- CCSS.Math.Content.6.EE.C.9
- CCSS.Math.Content.6.G.A.1
- CCSS.Math.Content.6.G.A.3

Prerequisite Skills

Prior to completing this unit, students should be proficient in the following mathematical skills: (Note: A practice sheet has been provided for each skill listed.)

- Writing equations to represent relationships between two variables in a given table
- Calculating the area of a quadrilateral
- Graphing polygons in a coordinate plane

Name: _____ Date: _____

Unit 4: The Mathematics of Educators

Prerequisite Skill Practice—Writing Equations

Directions: Write an equation that represents the relationship expressed in the table. The first problem has been worked out as an example.

1.

x	y
1	4
2	8
3	12
4	16
5	20

Because the value of the dependent variable (y) is the product of 4 and the value of the independent variable (x), the equation $y = 4x$ can be used to represent the relationship expressed in the table.

2.

a	b
1	3
2	6
3	9
4	12
5	15

3.

m	n
1	10
2	20
3	30
4	40
5	50

4.

p	q
1	9
2	18
3	27
4	36
5	45

5.

s	t
1	6
2	7
3	8
4	9
5	10

6.

y	z
1	11
2	12
3	13
4	14
5	15

7.

w	x
1	3
2	4
3	5
4	6
5	7

8.

f	g
1	8
2	9
3	10
4	11
5	12

Name: _____ Date: _____

Unit 4: The Mathematics of Educators

Prerequisite Skill Practice—Area of Rectangles

Directions: Calculate the area of the given rectangle. The first problem has been worked out as an example.

1. 6 in. 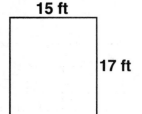 3 in. $A = bh$ $= (3 \text{ in.})(6 \text{ in.})$ $= 18 \text{ in.}^2$ The area of the rectangle is 18 square inches.	**2.** 12 cm 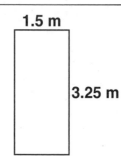 9 cm
3. 15 ft 17 ft	**4.** 1.5 m 3.25 m
5. 1.24 m 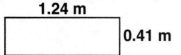 0.41 m	**6.** 5.3 yd 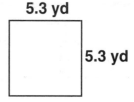 5.3 yd
7. 68 cm 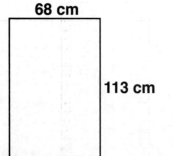 113 cm	**8.** 245 mm 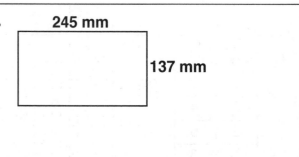 137 mm

Name: _____ Date: _____

Unit 4: The Mathematics of Educators

Prerequisite Skill Practice—Graphing Polygons

Directions: For each exercise, plot and connect the given points in the coordinate plane. Then identify the polygon that is formed. The first problem has been worked out as an example.

1.

A (–6, 7)
B (4, 7)
C (8, –2)
D (–2, –2)

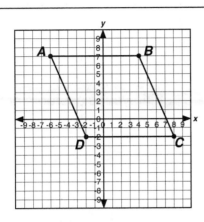

The figure is a parallelogram.

2.

Q (–6, –1)
R (0, –1)
S (0, –6)
T (–6, –6)

3.

W (2, 9)
X (5, 9)
Y (8, 0)
Z (1, 0)

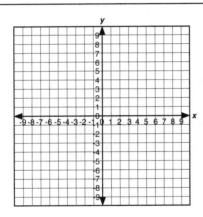

4.

L (–8, 10)
M (–3, 10)
N (–3, 2)
P (–8, 2)

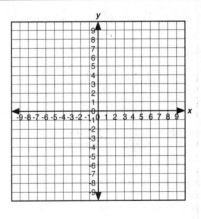

5.

D (0, 0)
E (6, 0)
F (5, –7)
G (1, –7)

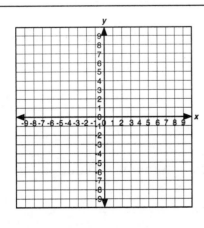

6.

J (–3, 3)
K (10, 3)
L (6, –8)
M (–7, –8)

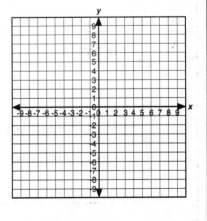

Name: _____ Date: _____

Unit 4: The Mathematics of Educators

Real-Life Application

The education profession is a very important one. We need good educators in our communities to educate and train the leaders of tomorrow. Whether you are a teacher, principal, superintendent or college professor, you will use mathematics. We will explore some of the mathematics that teachers use in this unit.

Organizing Supplies

Imagine that you are a public school teacher and are getting your classroom organized for the start of the school year.

1. The table shows the relationship between the number of students and the number of folders you need for the students.

Number of Students	Total Number of Folders
1	5
2	10
3	
4	20
	25
6	

a. Which quantity represents the independent variable? Explain how you determined your answer.

_____

_____

b. Which quantity represents the dependent variable? Explain how you determined your answer.

_____

_____

c. Describe the relationship between the independent and dependent variables.

_____

_____

Name: _____ Date: _____

Unit 4: The Mathematics of Educators

Real-Life Application (cont.)

d. Write an equation that represents the relationship between the independent and dependent variables. Let s represent the number of students and f represent the total number of folders.

_____

e. Use the equation you wrote in #1d to fill in the missing values in the table.

2. You plan to provide each student in your class with 4 pencils. Create a table that shows the relationship between the number of students and the total number of pencils.

3. Write an equation that represents the relationship between the number of students and the total number of pencils. Remember to define your variables first.

_____

_____

4. Use the equation from #3 to determine the number of pencils needed for a class of 23 students. Show your work.

_____

5. Pencils come in boxes of 30. How many boxes of pencils will you need to purchase to have enough for the students in your classroom? Explain how you determined your answer.

_____

_____

Name: _____ Date: _____

Unit 4: The Mathematics of Educators

Real-Life Application (cont.)

Decorating and Arranging Your Classroom

6. You decide to cover your bulletin board with blue material. The diagram below shows the dimensions of your board.

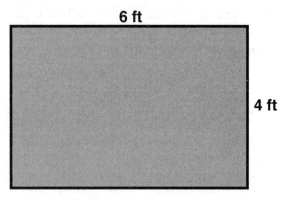

a. Calculate the amount of material you need to cover the bulletin board. Show your work.

_____

b. The material is 36 inches wide and is sold by the yard. How many yards of material do you need to buy in order to have enough to cover your entire bulletin board? Show your work.

_____

c. Will you have any material left over? Explain how you determined your answer.

_____

_____

Name: _____ Date: _____

Unit 4: The Mathematics of Educators

Real-Life Application (cont.)

7. You need to arrange the furniture around your classroom. You would like your desk at the back of the classroom and a table at the center of the front of the classroom. The custodians have requested that you provide a diagram of the arrangement of the furniture for your classroom so that they can place the pieces in the appropriate places after waxing the floors. The tile floors provide a nice grid for organizing the diagram. Each tile is 1 foot by 1 foot. You have painted *x*- and *y*-axes in the middle of your floor as shown on the grid below. One student desk has also been drawn on the grid. Your desk is 3 feet by 4 feet and the table is 2 feet by 6 feet.

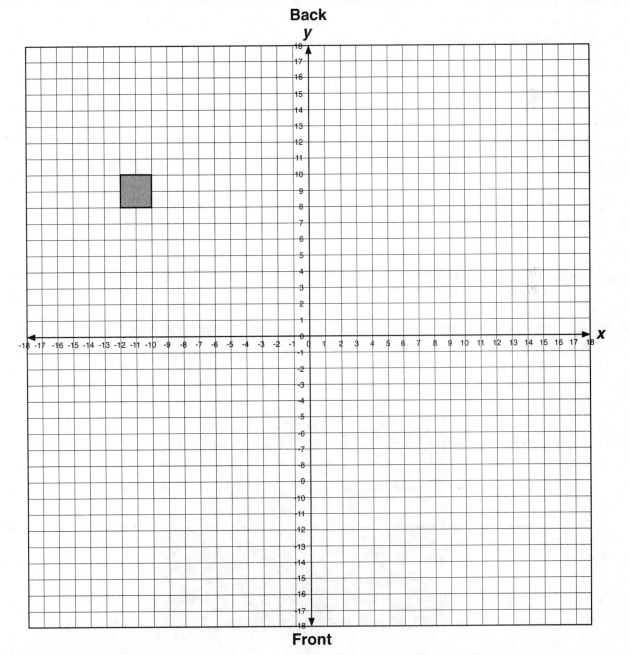

Name: _____ Date: _____

Unit 4: The Mathematics of Educators

Real-Life Application (cont.)

a. Draw your desk on the grid and give the coordinates for the corners of the desk.

_____

b. Draw the table on the grid and give the coordinates for the corners of the table. Remember that you would like for it to be placed in the center at the front.

_____

c. Use the coordinates of the corners of the student desk to determine the dimensions of the desk. Explain how you determined your answer.

_____

_____

_____

_____

d. You have 24 student desks in your classroom. One desk has already been drawn on the diagram. Draw in the other 23 desks so that the desks are spaced an equal distance apart.

Unit 5: The Mathematics of Law Enforcement

Introduction

Work in law enforcement is exciting, stressful, challenging, and rewarding. Police officers, private investigators, Drug Enforcement Administration (DEA) agents, and air marshals must all possess a wide range of knowledge and a variety of skills, including mathematics. Basic arithmetic, equation solving, probability and statistics, and geometry are some of the mathematical skills needed to succeed in law enforcement. The median annual salary for a police officer is $56,980.

Keeping the roads safe is something police officers do regularly. Police monitor roads for people driving recklessly. They issue fines that generate revenue that can be used to help keep roads safer for everyone. These tasks require the ability to quickly perform accurate mathematical calculations, making math an important part of traffic safety.

Law enforcement officers use statistics for a variety of reasons. Gathering and analyzing data help determine the best way to allocate resources in a patrol area. Concepts such as mean, median, box plots, and histograms help identify potentially disturbing trends. Understanding these and other statistical tools helps law enforcement officers effectively protect the public.

Police involvement in community activities helps everyone feel safe. Providing ample security for concerts and clearly explaining crime statistics to middle-school students are some ways in which law enforcement officers interact with the public. Solid math skills are required to effectively carry out such tasks.

These are just some of the ways mathematics is used in law enforcement and will be the focus of this unit as students explore the math used on the job in law enforcement careers.

Common Core State Standards

This unit addresses the following Common Core State Standards:

- CCSS.Math.Content.6.RP.A.3
- CCSS.Math.Content.6.G.A.1
- CCSS.Math.Content.6.SP.B.4
- CCSS.Math.Content.6.SP.B.5

Prerequisite Skills

Prior to completing this unit, students should be proficient in the following mathematical skills: (Note: A practice sheet has been provided for each skill listed.)

- Solving problems involving ratios and proportions
- Calculating statistical quantities
- Calculating values involving percent

Name: _____ Date: _____

Unit 5: The Mathematics of Law Enforcement

Prerequisite Skill Practice—Ratios and Proportions

Directions: Complete each exercise as directed. Show your work. The first problem has been worked out as an example.

1. How many of the 736 students in a middle school are teenagers if 3 out of every 8 students are teenagers? $\dfrac{3}{8} = \dfrac{x}{736}$ $736 \cdot 3 = 8 \cdot x$ $2{,}208 = 8x$ $x = 2{,}208 \div 8$ There are 276 $x = 276$ teenagers.	**2.** Determine the value of c (write your answer as a mixed number). $\dfrac{c}{28} = \dfrac{15}{44}$
3. There are 140 drivers on Main Street, 112 of which are male. What is the ratio of female to male drivers on Main Street?	**4.** Determine the value of a (write your answer as a decimal). $\dfrac{18}{a} = \dfrac{5}{14}$
5. Determine the value of n (write your answer as a mixed number). $\dfrac{11}{6} = \dfrac{n}{10}$	**6.** The ratio of demonstrators to police officers at a rally is 750:1. How many police officers are present if there are 16,500 demonstrators at the rally?
7. A police department issues new uniforms in a ratio of 8 shirts for every 5 pairs of pants. How many pairs of pants are issued if the police department issues 72 shirts?	**8.** Determine the value of x. $\dfrac{8}{15} = \dfrac{7}{x}$

Name: _____   Date: _____

Unit 5: The Mathematics of Law Enforcement

Prerequisite Skill Practice—Statistical Quantities

Directions: Use the given data to complete each exercise. Show your work. Write each answer as a simplified fraction or mixed number. The first problem has been worked out as an example.

$$10 \quad 13 \quad 14 \quad 17 \quad 18 \quad 19 \quad 19 \quad 21 \quad 22$$

1. Calculate the mean. $$\dfrac{10 + 13 + 14 + 17 + 18 + 19 + 19 + 21 + 22}{9}$$ $$= \dfrac{153}{9}$$ $$= 17$$ The mean of the data is 17.	**2.** Determine the mode, if any.
3. Calculate the range.	**4.** Determine the median.
5. Determine the first quartile.	**6.** Determine the third quartile.
7. Calculate the interquartile range.	**8.** Calculate the mean absolute deviation.

Name: _____ Date: _____

Unit 5: The Mathematics of Law Enforcement

Prerequisite Skill Practice—Percents

Directions: Complete each exercise as directed. Show your work. Be sure to label your final answers. The first problem has been worked out as an example.

1. What is 84% of 270? $0.84 \cdot 270 = 226.8$	**2.** 35% of what number is 98?
3. What percent of 32 is 76?	**4.** What is 216% of 153?
5. Odd numbers comprise what percent of the following values? 1 1 2 3 5 8 13 21 34 55 89 144 233 377 610 987	**6.** What is the total amount paid for a bicycle that costs $2,249.00 if sales tax is 6%?
7. The ratio of boys to girls in a middle school is 2:3. What percent of students in the school are girls?	**8.** What is the sale price of an item marked 30% off if the original price was $42.50?

Name: _____ Date: _____

Unit 5: The Mathematics of Law Enforcement

Real-Life Application

Law enforcement officers take on a variety of tasks each day while upholding their oath to serve and protect the public. Mathematics is required to effectively carry out many of their duties. In this unit, we will explore some of the mathematics Officer Maria Hernandez uses to carry out various tasks she encounters on the job as a police officer.

Traffic Enforcement

One of the most common duties of a police officer is to ensure the safety of motorists, cyclists, pedestrians, and everyone else on the roads in a given patrol area. Noticing when people break the law and correcting their behavior are essential to keeping the streets safe. The questions in this section relate to Officer Hernandez's work on traffic duty in her town.

1. Park Road has a posted speed limit of 40 mph but is notorious for being traveled by motorists driving well above the speed limit. Officer Hernandez records the following data to study the driving habits of motorists on Park Road in one day:

Speed (in mph)	40 & under	41-45	46-50	51-55	56-60	61-65	66 & over
Number of Vehicles	60	80	50	20	20	5	15

Construct a histogram for this data.

Name: _____ Date: _____

Unit 5: The Mathematics of Law Enforcement

Real-Life Application (cont.)

2. Use the data from #1 to determine the percentage of drivers who travel up to 10 mph above the posted speed limit on Park Road. Explain how you determined your answer.

_____

_____

3. Anyone traveling more than 25 mph above the posted speed limit is considered a reckless driver in Officer Hernandez's town. Based on the data in #1, how many out of every 1,000 drivers traveling on Park Road are expected to be reckless drivers? Show your work.

_____

4. Fines for speeding in Officer Hernandez's town are as follows: $100 for driving up to 10 mph over the speed limit; $175 for driving 11 to 25 mph over the speed limit; and $350 for driving more than 25 mph above the speed limit. How much would be collected in fines if each person speeding during Officer Hernandez's study were ticketed? Show your work.

_____

Name: _____ Date: _____

Unit 5: The Mathematics of Law Enforcement

Real-Life Application (cont.)

Youth Outreach

A very important aspect of law enforcement is serving as a role model for the community. Involvement in community outreach activities is an effective way to interact with citizens. The questions in this section pertain to Officer Hernandez's work with youth in her patrol area.

5. Officer Hernandez's town participates in a police ride-along program for high school students. Last year, 14 students participated in the program. The number of hours each student rode with a police officer is as follows:

12   17   19   20   21   21   21   25   28   31   34   35   38   42

a. Construct a box plot to summarize this information.

b. Calculate the mean number of hours each participating student rode with a police officer last year in the local ride-along program.

_____

45

Name: _____ Date: _____

Unit 5: The Mathematics of Law Enforcement

Real-Life Application (cont.)

6. Officer Hernandez is active in the Drug Abuse Resistance Education (D.A.R.E.) program. She visits five different schools in the region each month over a span of six months. What percentage of the 96 schools in the region will Officer Hernandez visit if she never visits the same school more than once? Explain how you determined your answer.

_____

_____

_____

Event Security

When a large gathering takes place, law enforcement officers are often called upon to provide security. Officer Hernandez's town has a convention center that often hosts events requiring this type of security. The questions in this section relate to Officer Hernandez's experiences working security detail during major events in her town.

7. The organizers of a political convention to be hosted in Officer Hernandez's town require one security officer to supervise every 300 square feet of space during the event. The convention center measures 85 feet by 147 feet. How many security officers must be on duty to ensure adequate coverage during the event? Use mathematics to support your answer.

_____

Name: _____   Date: _____

Unit 5: The Mathematics of Law Enforcement

Real-Life Application (cont.)

8. A comedy show at the convention center seats 1,240 audience members. Local regulations require a minimum of three security officers for every 100 spectators. Determine how many security officers are required to be on duty for the comedy show, and explain how you determined your answer.

_____

_____

_____

9. Police officers working security detail at the convention center are paid their overtime rate of time-and-a-half, which means they are paid 50% more than their regular hourly rate. Officer Hernandez normally earns $28.34 per hour. How much does she get paid for working a 7-hour shift as a security officer at the convention center in her town?

_____

_____

Unit 6: The Mathematics of Bankers

Introduction

Bankers are influential citizens in any community. Aside from counting money, bankers spend a lot of time with customers, calculating investment values and risks, and juggling a number of different accounts at once. There are many different roles that a banker can take, such as a personal banker, bank teller, or investment banker. A personal banker makes an average of $35,000 per year, as well as additional performance-based bonuses.

An important aspect of a banker's job is establishing trust with individual clients. Clients have to be confident that their banker is closely monitoring their money and making sound banking decisions. Demonstrating strong mathematical skills is very important in building this trust.

Bankers use mathematics in a variety of ways, such as analyzing accounts by assessing the impact of credits/deposits and debits/withdrawals on account balances. Bankers want to ensure that all of their clients maintain a positive balance, which means that they have money in their account. If their account has a negative balance, the client has spent more money than what is in their account. Then the client goes into debt. A banker's goal is to warn their clients and help them make better decisions before this happens.

These are just some of the ways mathematics is used by bankers and will be the focus of this unit as students explore the math needed to adequately manage money.

Common Core State Standards

This unit addresses the following Common Core State Standards:

- CCSS.Math.Content.6.RP.A.3C
- CCSS.Math.Content.6.NS.C.5
- CCSS.Math.Content.6.NS.C.7B
- CCSS.Math.Content.6.NS.C.7C
- CCSS.Math.Content.6.NS.C.7D

Prerequisite Skills

Prior to completing this unit, students should be proficient in the following mathematical skills: (Note: A practice sheet has been provided for each skill listed.)

- Using positive and negative numbers to represent quantities
- Comparing positive and negative numbers
- Solving problems with percents

Name: _____ Date: _____

Unit 6: The Mathematics of Bankers

Prerequisite Skill Practice—Integers in the Real World

Directions: For each of the following, write an integer to represent the value in the situation. The first problem has been done as an example.

1. A scuba diver is 65 feet below the surface. −65	**2.** A mountain climber is 9,650 feet above sea level.
3. The car is parked 5 levels under the ground.	**4.** The investor lost $585 in the stock market.
5. In July, the temperature was 83°F.	**6.** In January, the temperature was 12 degrees below zero.
7. Louie deposited $98 into his bank account.	**8.** Ben lost 15 yards on the football play.
9. A shipwreck was discovered 1,700 feet deep in the ocean.	**10.** Elena spent $14 at the candy store.

Name: _____ Date: _____

Unit 6: The Mathematics of Bankers

Prerequisite Skill Practice—Which One Is Greater?

Directions: For each of the following, determine the greater value. Write an inequality statement comparing the amounts. The first problem has been worked out as an example.

1. The height of the city of Badwater, California, is 282 feet below sea level. The height of the city of New Orleans, Lousiana, is 7 feet below sea level. The height of New Orleans has the greater value. $-7 > -282$	2. Jerome gained 6 yards on his first running play but lost 8 yards on his second running play.
3. In January, the average temperature in Mongolia is $-15°C$. In February, the average temperature is $-12°C$.	4. I lost \$12 on Tuesday. I found \$3 on Wednesday.
5. The boiling point of water is $0°C$. The boiling point of chloroform is $-63.5°C$.	6. The submarine is currently at -800 feet. The scuba diver is currently at -25 feet.
7. Jeff's golf score was 3 shots below par. Damon's golf score was 1 shot below par.	8. Saundra has \$233 in her account. Lina's account is \$238 in debt.

Name: _____ Date: _____

Unit 6: The Mathematics of Bankers

Prerequisite Skill Practice—Percent Problems

Directions: Answer each of the percent problems below. Show your work. The first problem has been worked out as an example.

1. 18 is 40% of what number? $\dfrac{18}{x} = \dfrac{40}{100}$ $\dfrac{18}{x} = \dfrac{2}{5}$ Multiply 18 · 5, $\dfrac{18}{45} = \dfrac{2}{5}$ and divide by 2. $x = 45$ 18 is 40% of 45.	**2.** 8 is what percent of 20?
3. What is 20% of 45?	**4.** 18 is 75% of what number?
5. What is 15% of 200?	**6.** What percent of 56 is 14?
7. What is 75% of 120?	**8.** 15 is what percent of 300?

Name: _____ Date: _____

Unit 6: The Mathematics of Bankers

Real-Life Application

A personal banker works with individuals to help them manage their bank accounts. Part of that is helping clients monitor their bank accounts, some of which have a negative balance or debt, which means that their bank account is less than $0. Others have a positive balance, which means that their bank account is greater than $0. In this unit, we will explore some of the mathematics bankers use.

Comparing Balances

Mr. Jones is a personal banker working with the following clients.

Client	Current Bank Balance (dollars)
Mr. McConnell	−35
Ms. Wohl	475
Ms. Abdous	−375
Mr. Kozlova	−598
Mr. Augustine	145
Ms. Moiamedi	15
Mr. Lundell	415
Ms. Mauger	−145

1. For each pair of clients, identify which client has a balance that is closer to $0 and write an inequality that compares the clients' balances.

a. Mr. McConnell and Ms. Moiamedi

_____

_____

b. Mr. Kozlova and Ms. Abdous

_____

_____

Name: _____ Date: _____

Unit 6: The Mathematics of Bankers

Real-Life Application (cont.)

c. Mr. Augustine and Ms. Mauger

_____

_____

d. Ms. Wohl and Mr. Lundell

_____

_____

e. Mr. Mauger and Ms. Abdous

_____

_____

2. Which of Mr. Jones' clients has the largest balance? Explain how you determined your answer.

_____

_____

3. Which of Mr. Jones' clients has the largest debt? Explain how you determined your answer.

_____

_____

4. Use words to explain how you can compare bank balances.

_____

_____

_____

Name: _____ Date: _____

Unit 6: The Mathematics of Bankers

Real-Life Application (cont.)

Credits and Debits

Becoming a bank teller is an entry-level introduction to the banking business. Bank tellers work with clients who walk into the bank to deposit or withdraw money from their account. Deposits (what you put into the account) are called *credits*, and withdrawals (what you take out of the account) are called *debits*. Bank tellers have to monitor all of the money that is exchanged throughout the day.

5. Mr. Garman is a bank teller, and at the end of the day, he has the following record of activity. For each of the following, use integers to represent the deposit or withdrawal.

Bank Activity	Integer Representation
Deposit of $450	
Debit of $135	
Credit of $99	
Withdrawal of $75	
Deposit of $3,525	
Credit of $429	
Withdrawal of $1,050	
Debit of $750	

6. One of Mr. Garman's responsibilities is to check his credits and debits and ensure that he has recorded them correctly. As he looks over this work one afternoon, he finds some mistakes. For each of the following, identify whether or not the credits and debits were entered correctly. Fix any mistakes by recording the values correctly.

Entry		Correct? (Y/N)	Corrected Value
Debit of $55	55		
Credit of $469	469		
Credit of $947.25	−947.25		
Debit of $64.75	64.75		
Debit of $777	−777		
Credit of $129.50	−129.50		
Credit of $57.50	57.50		

Name: _____   Date: _____

Unit 6: The Mathematics of Bankers

Real-Life Application (cont.)

7. In #6, how is the number in each mistake similar to the number in the correction? How is it different?

_____

_____

_____

Investment Banking

Unlike personal bankers or bank tellers, investment bankers work in the sale or merger of businesses. An investment banker manages the entire sale process, working hard to increase the value of the sale. This is important because investment bankers earn a fee or commission from their investments, and this is calculated as a percentage of the sale. The more money a banker can earn for a client, the more s/he will earn as well.

8. Ms. Toomey is an investment banker whose brokerage earns a 5% commission on sales. If she helped to sell a company that is worth $350,000, what is her commission? Show your work.

_____

9. Ms. O'Sullivan helped to merge two companies. The merger was worth $1,500,000, and her brokerage earned $52,500. What is the percent commission earned by this sale? Show your work.

_____

Name: _____ Date: _____

Unit 6: The Mathematics of Bankers

Real-Life Application (cont.)

Lending Money at Interest

The job of a banker that most people are familiar with is lending money. Bankers lend money to individuals or businesses that apply for loans. But the money isn't free. The loan has to be paid back with interest added on. This interest is calculated as a percentage of the original loan.

10. Suppose Hailey borrows $7,500 and has to pay 12% interest on her loan. How much interest will the bank charge her? Show your work.

_____

11. Sasha wants to borrow $12,000. If her banker tells her that she will owe $1,125 in interest when she pays back her loan, what is the percent interest that she is paying? Show your work.

_____

Unit 7: The Mathematics of Veterinarians

Introduction

Veterinarians are doctors who treat animals. Most veterinarians focus their care on large, small, or exotic animals. In addition to completing four years of college, a veterinarian must complete four years of veterinary school. Some of them also go on to complete a one-year internship or a two- to three-year residency that will lead to a board certification in an area of specialty. On average, a veterinarian earns between $90,000 and $100,000 per year.

Veterinarians provide well-animal care such as vaccinations and physicals, as well as sick-animal care and surgeries. Veterinarians must be both intelligent and compassionate in order to provide proper care to their patients.

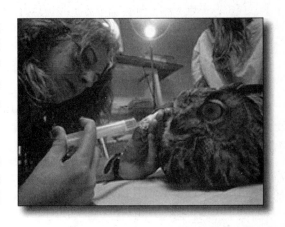

Veterinarians use mathematics on a daily basis in order to calculate the correct dosages for medicines and vaccines, and to monitor the health of their patients by charting pet growth. Further, veterinarians need to be able to use statistics to assess their clients' needs and improve customer service.

These are just some of the ways mathematics is used by veterinarians and will be the focus of this unit as students explore the math needed to provide professional care to animals.

Common Core State Standards

This unit addresses the following Common Core State Standards:

- CCSS.Math.Content.6.RP.A.2
- CCSS.Math.Content.6.RP.A.3a
- CCSS.Math.Content.6.RP.A.3d
- CCSS.Math.Content.6.NS.B.3
- CCSS.Math.Content.6.NS.C.8
- CCSS.Math.Content.6.EE.B.6

- CCSS.Math.Content.6.EE.B.7
- CCSS.Math.Content.6.EE.C.9
- CCSS.Math.Content.6.SP.A.1
- CCSS.Math.Content.6.SP.B.4
- CCSS.Math.Content.6.SP.B.5b

Prerequisite Skills

Prior to completing this unit, students should be proficient in the following mathematical skills: (Note: A practice sheet has been provided for each skill listed.)

- Writing equations to represent a situation
- Identifying good statistical questions and the attributes they measure
- Graphing a data set in a coordinate plane

Name: _____ Date: _____

Unit 7: The Mathematics of Veterinarians

Prerequisite Skill Practice—Writing Equations

Directions: Write an equation to represent the given relationship. The first problem has been done as an example.

1. One yard is equal to three feet. Write an equation that can be used to convert yards to feet. Be sure to define your variables. Let y represent yards and f represent feet. Then, $f = 3y$	**2.** Four quarts is equal to one gallon. Write an equation that can be used to convert gallons to quarts. Be sure to define your variables.
3. One centimeter is equal to 10 millimeters. Write an equation that can be used to convert centimeters to millimeters. Be sure to define your variables.	**4.** Sixteen ounces is equal to one pound. Write an equation that can be used to convert pounds to ounces. Be sure to define your variables.
5. One inch is approximately equal to 2.54 centimeters. Write an equation that can be used to convert inches to centimeters. Be sure to define your variables.	**6.** One Euro is approximately equal to 1.127 United States dollars. Write an equation that can be used to convert Euros to dollars. Be sure to define your variables.
7. One liter is approximately equal to 0.264 gallon. Write an equation that can be used to convert liters to gallons. Be sure to define your variables.	**8.** One pound on Earth is approximately equal to 0.17 pound on the moon. Write an equation that can be used to convert pounds on Earth to pounds on the moon. Be sure to define your variables.

Name: _____ Date: _____

Unit 7: The Mathematics of Veterinarians

Prerequisite Skill Practice—Statistical Questions

Directions: Determine whether or not the given question is a good statistical question. If it is, identify the attribute being measured and the unit used to measure it. If it is not, explain why not. The first problem has been done as an example.

1. How many cousins do my classmates have? This is a good statistical question because it allows for variability. The attribute being measured is number of cousins. It is measured in people.
2. How many cousins do I have?
3. On a scale of 1 to 10, with 1 being strongly dislike and 10 being strongly like, rate how much you like school.
4. How many years have my teammates played soccer?
5. What is my shoe size?
6. How old are the teachers in my school?

Name: _____ Date: _____

Unit 7: The Mathematics of Veterinarians

Prerequisite Skill Practice—Graphing Data Sets

Directions: Create a line graph for the data set. The first problem has been completed for you as an example.

1.

Time (hours)	1	2	3	4	5	6	7	8	9	10
Temperature (°C)	23	25	29	29	30	30	31	28	26	22

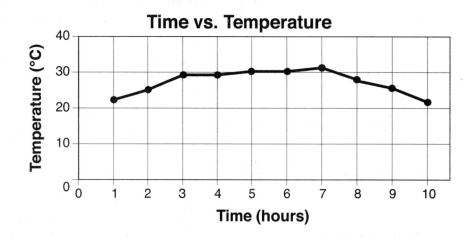

2.

Days	1	2	3	4	5	6	7	8	9	10
Distance (miles)	3	5	2	2	3	6	5	5	6	5

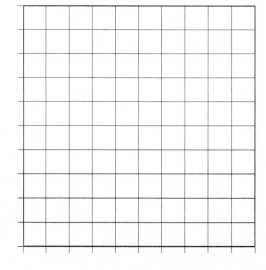

Name: _____ Date: _____

Unit 7: The Mathematics of Veterinarians

Real-Life Application

If you love working with and caring for animals, then a career in veterinary medicine might be the thing for you. As with most jobs, there is some mathematics involved in being a veterinarian, and we will explore some of those mathematic concepts in this unit.

Conversions Used by Veterinarians

Veterinarians use three systems of measurements—metric, apothecary, and household. They must calculate within and between these systems accurately so that they can give their furry patients appropriate dosages of medication. Imagine that you are a veterinarian and are treating a variety of canine patients. Use the dosage chart below to calculate the proper doses.

Product	Canine dosage	Used to…
Buffered aspirin	5 mg per pound every 12 hours	reduce inflammation and relieve pain
Benadryl	Up to 2 mg per pound every 8 hours	treat allergies and itching
Amoxicillin	5 mg per pound every 12 hours	treat bacterial infections
Ampicillin	10 mg per pound every 8 hours	treat bacterial infections
Tetracycline	10 mg per pound every 6 hours	treat bacterial infections

1. A dog named Jack comes into your office, and you discern that he has a bacterial infection. The dog weighs 12 kilograms.

   a. One kilogram is approximately equivalent to 2.2 pounds. Determine how many pounds Jack weighs. Show your work.

   _____

   b. Use your answer to #1a to help you write an equation that can be used to convert any dog's weight from kilograms to pounds. Be sure to define your variables.

   _____

   _____

Name: _____ Date: _____

Unit 7: The Mathematics of Veterinarians

Real-Life Application (cont.)

2. You decide to treat Jack's bacterial infection with amoxicillin.

    a. How many milligrams of amoxicillin should Jack's owner give every 12 hours? Show your work.

_____

    b. You want Jack to take the medication for 10 days. How many milligrams of amoxicillin will you need to send home with Jack's owner so that he'll have the correct amount needed for 10 days? Show your work and explain how you determined your answer.

_____

_____

_____

3. Your next canine patient is a dog named Cleo. She weighs 7.5 kilograms and also has a bacterial infection. You decide to treat Cleo's infection with tetracycline for 8 days.

    a. Use the equation you wrote in #1b to calculate Cleo's weight in pounds. Show your work.

_____

    b. How much tetracycline will Cleo's owner need in order to be able to give her the proper dosage for 8 days? Show your work and explain how you determined your answer.

_____

_____

_____

Name: _____ Date: _____

Unit 7: The Mathematics of Veterinarians

Real-Life Application (cont.)

Charting Canine Growth

As a veterinarian, one of your roles is to monitor the growth of your furry patients to ensure their healthy development. The table below shows the weights for your patient, Belle, at different ages.

Age (weeks)	Weight (pounds)	Age (weeks)	Weight (pounds)
4	5	32	51
8	11	36	53
12	17	40	58
16	26	44	62
20	34	48	63
24	39	52	63
28	47	56	63

4. Make a line graph of the data in the table. Graph the age on the *x*-axis and the weight on the *y*-axis.

5. Explain what the graph shows about Belle's growth over 56 weeks.

_____

_____

Name: _____ Date: _____

Unit 7: The Mathematics of Veterinarians

Real-Life Application (cont.)

6. Between weeks 4 and 8, Belle grew 6 pounds.

a. Determine the unit rate of growth for Belle between weeks 4 and 8. Show your work.

_____

b. If Belle continued to grow at this rate, explain what that would mean for her growth.

_____

_____

_____

c. Complete the table below to show Belle's growth if she continued to grow at the unit rate you calculated in #6a.

Age (weeks)	Weight (pounds)	Age (weeks)	Weight (pounds)
4	5	13	
5		14	
6		15	
7		16	
8		17	
9		18	
10		19	
11		20	
12			

d. Add Belle's projected growth as determined in #6c to the line graph you made in #4.

e. Write an equation that represents the relationship between Belle's age, in weeks, and her weight, in pounds, using the unit growth rate.

_____

Name: _____ Date: _____

Unit 7: The Mathematics of Veterinarians

Real-Life Application (cont.)

f. Use the equation from #6e to predict how much Belle will weigh when she is 56 weeks old. Does your answer seem reasonable? Explain why or why not.

_____

_____

_____

Customer Service

7. You decide to survey your clients to see if there is a way for you to improve their experiences at your clinic. You create the following survey for them to complete at the end of each visit.

Client Survey

1. What kind of pet did you bring to the clinic for treatment today?

2. Were you satisfied with the care provided at your visit today?

3. Circle the option below that best indicates the number of years you have been our client.

    Less than 1   1 to 3   3 to 5   5 to 7   More than 7

---

a. Are all of your survey questions good statistical questions? Explain your reasoning.

_____

_____

_____

b. Write an additional question for your client survey. Identify the unit of measure that will be used to describe the attribute measured by your question.

_____

_____

_____

Unit 8: The Mathematics of Computer Programming

Introduction

Whether writing code for video games, developing business software, or updating a social networking interface, computer programming relies heavily on mathematics. Programmers earn a median annual salary of $74,280. Arithmetic is necessary for spreadsheets, geometry is essential to computer-aided design (CAD), and trigonometry is a fundamental tool for animation. Nearly every aspect of computer programming requires at least some math. This unit will focus on some of the mathematics involved in writing code for video games.

Many video games provide players opportunities to advance to higher levels by solving puzzles and overcoming challenges to earn rewards. These games often pose challenges and offer rewards corresponding to a player's level of experience. Basic arithmetic, including order of operations, can be used to determine appropriate challenges and rewards for game players.

Drawing figures on a computer screen is a necessary part of many video games. In computing, these figures are little more than collections of polygons, primarily triangles. Understanding geometry, particularly polygons, allows figures in video games to be seen properly.

Animated graphics make many video games more fun and exciting for players. Among other tools, animation requires manipulating equations to position graphics on a coordinate plane that represents the computer screen. Algebraic concepts, including solving equations and plotting points, are needed to animate figures on the screen.

These are just some of the ways mathematics is used in computer programming and will be the focus of this unit as students explore the math used in computing.

Common Core State Standards

This unit addresses the following Common Core State Standards:

- CCSS.Math.Content.6.NS.C.6
- CCSS.Math.Content.6.NS.C.8
- CCSS.Math.Content.6.EE.A.1
- CCSS.Math.Content.6.EE.A.2

- CCSS.Math.Content.6.EE.B.7
- CCSS.Math.Content.6.EE.C.9
- CCSS.Math.Content.6.G.A.2
- CCSS.Math.Content.6.G.A.3

Prerequisite Skills

Prior to completing this unit, students should be proficient in the following mathematical skills: (Note: A practice sheet has been provided for each skill listed.)

- Calculating values involving rational numbers
- Writing and solving basic algebraic equations
- Determining coordinates, area, and volume of geometric figures

Name: _____   Date: _____

Unit 8: The Mathematics of Computer Programming

Prerequisite Skill Practice—Operations With Rational Numbers

Directions: Complete each exercise as indicated. Show your work. The first problem has been worked out as an example.

1. $5\frac{1}{2} \cdot 3\frac{1}{5}$ $5\frac{1}{2} \cdot 3\frac{1}{5} = \frac{11}{\cancel{2}_{1}} \cdot \frac{\cancel{16}^{8}}{5}$ $= \frac{88}{5}$ or $17\frac{3}{5}$	2. $\frac{3}{4} - \frac{5}{6}$
3. $\quad 3^7$	4. $\left(-1\frac{2}{5}\right) - \left(-6\frac{2}{3}\right)$
5. $\quad 6\frac{7}{8} \div \frac{5}{16}$	6. $22\frac{7}{10} + \left(-11\frac{1}{2}\right)$
7. $5\frac{1}{4} - \left(-3\frac{7}{8}\right)$	8. $\left(\frac{2}{5}\right)^4$

Name: _____ Date: _____

Unit 8: The Mathematics of Computer Programming

Prerequisite Skill Practice—Algebraic Equations

Directions: Complete each exercise as indicated. Show your work. The first problem has been worked out as an example.

1. Solve the following equation: $$x + 14 = 5$$ $$\begin{array}{r} x + \cancel{14} = 5 \\ -\ \cancel{14} \quad -14 \\ \hline x = -9 \end{array}$$	2. A computer downloads 30 megabits per second for t seconds. Write an equation to represent the number of Megabits, m, downloaded.
3. Solve the following equation: $$4y = 30$$	4. Solve the following equation: $$n + 5\tfrac{1}{4} = 12\tfrac{2}{3}$$
5. Solve the following equation: $$\tfrac{4}{9}b = 2\tfrac{3}{5}$$	6. A teenager has $3\tfrac{1}{2}$ hours left before reaching his total number of hours, t, of online time allowed for the week. Write an equation for t in terms of the number of hours, h, the teenager has already been online for the week.
7. Solve the following equation: $$x + \tfrac{3}{10} = \tfrac{1}{4}$$	8. Solve the following equation: $$\tfrac{5}{7}p = 70$$

Name: _____   Date: _____

Unit 8: The Mathematics of Computer Programming

Prerequisite Skill Practice—Geometric Calculations

Directions: Complete each exercise as indicated. Show your work. Use your own paper if you need more room. The first problem has been worked out as an example.

---

1. Determine the area of a rectangle that is $2\frac{1}{3}$ centimeters wide and $4\frac{1}{5}$ centimeters tall.

$A = lw$, so $\quad A = 2\frac{1}{3} \cdot 4\frac{1}{5}$

$$= \frac{7}{\cancel{3}_1} \cdot \frac{\cancel{21}^{7}}{5}$$

$$= \frac{49}{5} \text{ or } 9\frac{4}{5}$$

The rectangle has an area of $9\frac{4}{5}$ square centimeters.

2. Calculate the volume of a cube with side lengths $\frac{3}{4}$ inch.

---

3. Compute the distance between the points having coordinates $(-4, 2)$ and $(7, 2)$.

4. Calculate the area of a triangle with vertices located at $(-2, -3)$, $(4, -3)$, and $(4, 8)$.

---

5. Calculate the area of a triangle with vertices located at $(0, 0)$, $(0, 7)$, and $(9, 3)$.

6. Determine the volume of a box that is 2 feet long, $1\frac{1}{4}$ feet wide, and $\frac{2}{3}$ foot tall.

---

7. Calculate the distance from $(6, -18)$ to $(6, -3)$ in the coordinate plane.

8. Compute the area of a rectangle measuring $\frac{7}{8}$ meter by $6\frac{2}{5}$ meters.

Name: _____ Date: _____

Unit 8: The Mathematics of Computer Programming

Real-Life Application

      Computer programming relies heavily on mathematics regardless of the application under development. Whether manipulating geometric shapes, using logic to implement artificial intelligence, or simply carrying out basic arithmetic calculations, writing code requires a variety of mathematics skills. In this unit, we will explore some of the mathematics that may be encountered by computer programmers writing code for video games.

<u>Moving Objects</u>

1. Computer graphics are constructed by using a coordinate plane to represent the screen. Each individual dot on the screen, known as a *pixel* (short for "picture element"), represents one unit, and the origin, (0, 0), is usually located at the top-left corner, the bottom-left corner, or the center of the screen. For the questions below, assume the screen being used is 1,920 pixels wide and 1,200 pixels tall with the origin located at the center of the screen.

    a. Give the coordinates of each of the four corners of the screen. Explain how you determined your answer.

    _____

    _____

    _____

    b. An object on the screen is located at coordinates (389, −286) and is moving upward at a rate of 28 pixels per second. Determine which coordinate, *x* or *y*, is changing, and write an equation to give the value of that coordinate *t* seconds after the object starts moving. Explain how you determined your answer.

    _____

    _____

    _____

Name: _____ Date: _____

Unit 8: The Mathematics of Computer Programming

Real-Life Application (cont.)

c. A second object on the screen is located at coordinates (–325, 190) and is moving to the right at a rate of 42 pixels per second. Determine which coordinate, *x* or *y*, is changing, and write an equation to give the value of that coordinate *t* seconds after the object starts moving. Explain how you determined your answer.

_____

_____

_____

d. As the term implies, a "collision" in a video game occurs when two objects occupy the same point on a coordinate plane. Will the two objects described in #1b and #1c collide if they start moving at the same time? If so, how long after they start moving will the collision occur? If not, explain why. Use mathematics to support your answer.

_____

_____

_____

_____

Name: _____ Date: _____

Unit 8: The Mathematics of Computer Programming

Real-Life Application (cont.)

Earning Rewards

2. Some video games require players to complete tasks, solve puzzles, or defend themselves to gain experience in order to move up to higher levels or earn rewards used to acquire tools to help continue the adventure. As the game progresses, the challenges become harder, but the rewards become greater. The questions that follow pertain to such a video game.

a. The game requires players to build walls to defend their homes from invaders. A completed wall must have a width of $4\frac{1}{2}$ units, a height of 3 units, and a depth of $1\frac{1}{2}$ units in order to be effective. What is the volume of an effective wall?

_____

b. The building blocks used to construct the walls discussed in #2a are cubes measuring $\frac{1}{2}$ unit on each side. How many building blocks must be available for a player to construct an effective wall? Explain how you determined your answer.

_____

_____

_____

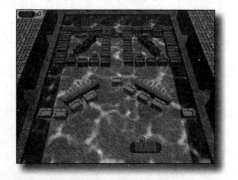

Unit 8: The Mathematics of Computer Programming

Real-Life Application (cont.)

c. Players can solve puzzles to earn tokens that can be used to purchase items that will help them progress through the game world, including the building blocks necessary to construct the defense wall. Each puzzle solved earns the player 20 tokens, and each block costs 3 tokens. If all tokens earned are used to purchase building blocks, how many puzzles must be solved to purchase all the building blocks necessary to construct an effective wall?

_____

Online Games

3. Online games appear in many varieties. Some online games allow players to interact with one another while progressing through the challenges presented by the game. A fictitious online game in which players collaborate with one another as heroes to defeat villains is the backdrop for the questions in this section.

a. A player begins a session of the online game and invites others to join him. Each time a new player joins the game, the number of villains to defeat throughout the game world doubles. If there are 2 villains when the first player starts the game, how many villains will there be after the fifth new player joins the game? Use mathematics to support your answer.

_____

_____

_____

_____

Name: _____ Date: _____

Unit 8: The Mathematics of Computer Programming

Real-Life Application (cont.)

b. Each player's computer screen shows the view from above of his or her character in the center of a rectangular grid displaying the game world for 75 feet in each direction. Rafael is online playing the game with Naoki and Sergei. Naoki's character is currently 28 feet directly behind Rafael's character. How far directly ahead of Naoki's character can Sergei's character be while still being displayed on Rafael's computer screen?

_____

_____

_____

c. In order to defeat the final villain in the game, Rafael, Naoki, and Sergei must position their characters in the shape of a right triangle. Because a player's character is centered on the screen as stated in #3b, his or her character can be considered to be located at the origin in a coordinate plane with each unit representing 1 foot. Give two possible ordered pairs to represent the location of Naoki's character on Rafael's computer screen if Sergei's character is located at (−23, −45) so the three characters form a right triangle. Explain how you determined your answer.

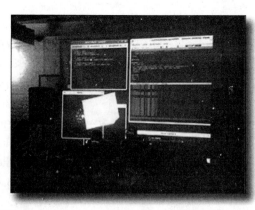

_____

_____

_____

Unit 9: The Mathematics of Air Traffic Controllers

Introduction

Air traffic controllers have a critical role in keeping the skies safe for the nearly 8 million people who fly on airplanes every day. Air traffic controllers are at work 24 hours per day coordinating the movement of airplanes to ensure that they stay at a safe distance from each other. The starting annual salary for this job is approximately $37,000, but the median annual wage is $122,530.

There are different types of air traffic controllers. *Tower controllers* ensure that planes are moving safely on the ground and give planes clearance to land or take off. *Approach and departure controllers* help airplanes maintain a safe distance from each other as they approach and depart from the airports. *En route controllers* monitor aircraft as they fly from one airport's airspace to another. All of these controllers must think quickly and clearly to ensure that all airplanes have correct information.

Air traffic controllers must use mental math with precision in order to communicate distances to aircraft and prevent them from getting too close together on the runways, during take-off and landings, and while they are in the air. Air traffic controllers do this by monitoring the altitude (height above the earth) and the speed of the airplanes. Any mistake in their calculations could cause airplanes to fly dangerously close together.

These are just some of the ways mathematics is used by air traffic controllers and will be the focus of this unit as students explore the math needed to keep air travel safe for all travelers.

Common Core State Standards

This unit addresses the following Common Core State Standards:

- CCSS.Math.Content.6.NS.B.4
- CCSS.Math.Content.6.EE.B.5
- CCSS.Math.Content.6.EE.B.6
- CCSS.Math.Content.6.EE.B.7
- CCSS.Math.Content.6.EE.C.9

Prerequisite Skills

Prior to completing this unit, students should be proficient in the following mathematical skills: (Note: A practice sheet has been provided for each skill listed.)

- Solving problems using the formula $d = rt$
- Writing and solving basic algebraic equations
- Using substitution to determine whether a given number makes an equation true

Name: _____   Date: _____

Unit 9: The Mathematics of Air Traffic Controllers

Prerequisite Skill Practice—Distance, Rate, and Time Problems

Directions: Solve each of the following problems using $d = rt$, where d represents distance, r represents the rate or speed, and t represents time. Show your work. The first problem has been worked out as an example.

1. An airplane flies 2,175 miles in 3 hours. What is the average speed of the airplane? $d = rt$ $2175 = 3r$ $2175 \div 3 = 3r \div 3$ $725 = r$ The average speed is 725 mph.	2. Finn is riding his bike at 8.5 miles per hour. How far can he go in 3 hours?
3. Anne rides her horse with a constant speed of 14 miles per hour. How far can she travel in $\frac{3}{4}$ hour?	4. Parker roller skates with a constant speed of 8 miles per hour. How long will he take to travel a distance of 12 miles?
5. An airplane flies with a constant speed of 780 miles per hour. How far can it travel in 3 hours?	6. Nora rides her bike 15 miles in $1\frac{1}{2}$ hours. What is her average speed?
7. Juan roller skates 9 miles in $1\frac{1}{4}$ hours. What is his average speed?	8. A train travels with a constant speed of 34 miles per hour. How long will it take to travel a distance of 51 miles?

Name: _____   Date: _____

Unit 9: The Mathematics of Air Traffic Controllers

Prerequisite Skill Practice—Algebraic Equations

Directions: For each of the following, write an addition equation and solve for the unknown. Show your work. The first problem has been worked out as an example.

1. 435 increased by a number is 500. What is that number? $$435 + x = 500$$ $$435 - 435 + x = 500 - 435$$ $$x = 65$$ That number is 65.	2. Martha had 45 likes on her profile picture before school. After school she had 63 likes. How many likes were added during the school day?
3. Last month, Kendra ran 30 miles more than Anthony. Kendra ran 47 miles. How many miles did Anthony run?	4. A number plus 17 is 29.5. What is the number?
5. Simeon had some money in his wallet. He put in $20 and now has $38 in his wallet. How much money was in his wallet originally?	6. Anne is driving 35 mph. She speeds up to 48 mph. By how much did her speed increase?
7. The sum of 68 and a number is 115. What is the number?	8. A number added to 785 is 993. What is the number?
9. 515 plus a number is 900. What is the number?	10. The oven temperature is 225°F, but it needs to heat to 400°F. How many degrees does the temperature need to increase?

Unit 9: The Mathematics of Air Traffic Controllers

Prerequisite Skill Practice—Substitute to Verify Equations

Directions: Use substitution to determine whether each equation is true for the given value of x. Show your work. The first problem has been worked out as an example.

1. $6x + 7 = 20 - 3x$; $x = 2$ $6(2) + 7 = 20 - 3(2)$ $12 + 7 = 20 - 6$ $19 = 14$ No, the equation is not true for this value of x.	**2.** $15 - 6x = 9$; $x = 1$
3. $\dfrac{x + 2}{x - 3} = 2$; $x = 8$	**4.** $4x - 4 = 0$; $x = 2$
5. $\dfrac{x - 5}{2} = \dfrac{x + 2}{3}$; $x = 19$	**6.** $4x - 6 = 6$; $x = 3$
7. $\dfrac{5x}{2} = 3x + 5$; $x = 3$	**8.** $2(3x - 4) = 3x + 1$; $x = 4$

Name: _____   Date: _____

Unit 9: The Mathematics of Air Traffic Controllers

Real-Life Application

Are you good at thinking under pressure? Do you like to do mathematics in your head? Air traffic controllers work under a great deal of pressure to make sure that all of the airplanes that travel every day arrive safely at their destinations. In this unit, we will explore some of the mathematics that air traffic controllers use on a daily basis.

Approach and Departure Controllers

Approach and departure controllers monitor aircraft as they approach and depart from an airport's airspace. They work to make sure that all aircraft maintain a safe distance from each other as they take off and land.

1. An approach controller is monitoring two aircraft that are traveling toward the airport. The first aircraft, UA2439, is traveling at 420 mph and is 126 miles from the airport. The second aircraft, WS745, is traveling 435 mph and is 145 miles from the airport.

   a. Write an equation that relates the speed and the distance that UA2439 is from the airport.

   _____

   b. Write an equation that relates the speed and the distance that WS745 is from the airport.

   _____

   c. If both aircraft maintain their current speeds, which aircraft will approach the airport first? Explain how you determined your answer and use mathematics to support it.

   _____

   _____

   _____

Name: _____   Date: _____

Unit 9: The Mathematics of Air Traffic Controllers

Real-Life Application (cont.)

d. The approach controller does not want the two planes arriving so close to each other, so she tells WS745 to slow down to 360 mph. How long will it now take flight WS745 to approach the airport?

_____

_____

2. When an aircraft is making its final approach to the airport, it must slow down in order to land safely. If it slows down to 145 mph for the final 15 minutes of the flight, how many miles will it cover in the final approach? (Hint: Remember to convert minutes to hours.)

_____

_____

Name: _____ Date: _____

Unit 9: The Mathematics of Air Traffic Controllers

Real-Life Application (cont.)

En Route Controllers

En route controllers take over monitoring aircraft once they have taken off and left the airport's airspace. Once flights get close to their destination airport, the en route controllers hand over control of the flight to an approach controller.

3. Flight DL685 is currently flying at an altitude of 34,550 feet. The en route controller needs the flight to ascend to 38,452 feet to create a safe distance from another aircraft. Write and solve an equation to determine how many feet the controller tells the pilot to ascend.

_____

_____

4. Flight VS522 is currently flying at an altitude of 6,500 feet and a speed of 250 miles per hour. Write and solve an equation to determine how long it will take the aircraft to travel the 560 miles to its destination at its current rate.

_____

_____

Name: _____   Date: _____

Unit 9: The Mathematics of Air Traffic Controllers

Real-Life Application (cont.)

5. The pilot of flight VS522 from #4 requests to climb to 11,500 feet with an increase in speed to 400 miles per hour.

   a. Write and solve an equation to represent the increase in altitude.

   _____

   _____

   b. Write and solve an equation to represent the increase in speed.

   _____

   _____

   c. If the en route controller approves the pilot's request and the plane covers 30 miles during the increase in speed, how long will it take the aircraft to travel the 530 miles remaining to its destination?

   _____

   _____

6. The pilot of flight SW778 requests to fly the 1,995 miles to his destination at a speed of 570 mph. The pilot has 3 hours to fly this distance. Is this a good plan? Substitute the values into $d = rt$ to determine if this plan will work.

   _____

   _____

   _____

Name: _____ Date: _____

Unit 9: The Mathematics of Air Traffic Controllers

Real-Life Application (cont.)

7. The air traffic controller tells the pilot of flight SW778 to fly the 1,995 miles at a speed of 665 mph. He says that this will take 3 hours. Is the air traffic controller correct? Substitute the values into $d = rt$ to determine if this plan will work.

_____

_____

_____

Tower Controllers

Tower controllers are responsible for controlling the paths of aircraft that are on the ground at the airport. Tower controllers direct aircraft to push back from the gate, tell pilots when they can safely take off, and guide the traffic on the runway.

8. A tower controller has 2 different airlines filling the gates of Terminal A at the airport. The first airline schedules a plane to push back from one of its gates every 6 minutes. The second airline schedules a plane to push back from one of its gates every 8 minutes. In how many minutes will the tower controller have 2 planes pushing back at the same time? Show your work.

_____

_____

9. At terminal E, a tower controller has 2 different airlines as well. One airline has scheduled planes to push back every 9 minutes, and the other airline has scheduled planes to push back every 10 minutes. In how many minutes will the tower controller have 2 planes pushing back at the same time? Show your work.

_____

_____

Answer Keys

Unit 1: Lemonade Stands
Ratios and Proportions (p. 3)

2) $\dfrac{2\frac{1}{4}}{1\frac{1}{2}} = \dfrac{9}{x} \rightarrow 2\frac{1}{4}x = 1\frac{1}{2} \cdot 9 \rightarrow \frac{9}{4}x = \frac{3}{2} \cdot \frac{9}{1} =$

$\frac{9}{4}x = \frac{27}{2} \rightarrow x = \dfrac{\overset{3}{\cancel{27}}}{2} \cdot \dfrac{\overset{2}{\cancel{4}}}{\underset{1}{\cancel{9}}} \rightarrow x = \frac{6}{1} \rightarrow x = 6$

6 cups of sugar

3) $\frac{n}{32} = \frac{9}{20} \rightarrow 20n = 288 \rightarrow n = 288 \div 20 \rightarrow$
$n = 14.4$

4) $\frac{8}{15} = \frac{x}{40} \rightarrow 320 = 15x \rightarrow x = 320 \div 15 \rightarrow$
$x = \frac{320}{15} \rightarrow x = \frac{64}{3} \rightarrow x = 21\frac{1}{3}$

5) $\frac{10}{3} = \frac{x}{42} \rightarrow 420 = 3x \rightarrow x = 420 \div 3 \rightarrow$
$x = 140$ 140 cars

6) $\frac{6}{a} = \frac{21}{34} \rightarrow 204 = 21a \rightarrow a = 204 \div 21 \rightarrow$
$a = \frac{204}{21} \rightarrow a = \frac{68}{7}$

7) $\frac{11}{19} = \frac{7}{c} \rightarrow 11c = 133 \rightarrow c = 133 \div 11 \rightarrow$
$c = \frac{133}{11}$ or $c = 12\frac{1}{11}$ or $c = 12.\overline{09}$

8) $\frac{5}{3} = \frac{x}{9} \rightarrow 45 = 3x \rightarrow x = 45 \div 3 \rightarrow x = 15$
15 consonants; $15 + 9 = 24$ letters

Operations with Rational Numbers (p. 4)

2) $7\frac{1}{5} \div 6\frac{3}{4} = \frac{36}{5} \div \frac{27}{4} = \dfrac{\overset{4}{\cancel{36}}}{5} \cdot \dfrac{4}{\underset{3}{\cancel{27}}} = \frac{16}{15}$ or $1\frac{1}{15}$

3) $12\frac{3}{4} \cdot 8\frac{1}{2} = \frac{51}{4} \cdot \frac{17}{2} = \frac{867}{8}$ or $108\frac{3}{8}$

4) $9\frac{3}{8} + 2\frac{5}{6} = 9\frac{9}{24} + 2\frac{20}{24} = 11\frac{29}{24} = 12\frac{5}{24}$

5) $12\frac{1}{2} \div 4\frac{1}{6} = \frac{25}{2} \div \frac{25}{6} = \dfrac{\cancel{25}}{\underset{1}{\cancel{2}}} \cdot \dfrac{\overset{3}{\cancel{6}}}{\underset{1}{\cancel{25}}} = \frac{3}{1} = 3$

6) $\frac{4}{7} \cdot 2\frac{1}{10} = \dfrac{4}{\underset{1}{\cancel{7}}} \cdot \dfrac{\overset{3}{\cancel{21}}}{\underset{5}{\cancel{10}}} = \frac{6}{5}$ or $1\frac{1}{5}$

7) $10\frac{7}{12} + 1\frac{2}{3} = 10\frac{7}{12} + 1\frac{8}{12} = 11\frac{15}{12} = 12\frac{3}{12} = 12\frac{1}{4}$

8) $7\frac{3}{4} - 2\frac{5}{6} = 7\frac{9}{12} - 2\frac{10}{12} = 6\frac{21}{12} - 2\frac{10}{12} = 4\frac{11}{12}$

9) $\frac{7}{8} - \frac{7}{9} = \frac{63}{72} - \frac{56}{72} = \frac{7}{72}$

10) $4\frac{3}{8} \div \frac{2}{5} = \frac{35}{8} \div \frac{2}{5} = \frac{35}{8} \cdot \frac{5}{2} = \frac{175}{16}$ or $10\frac{15}{16}$

Working with Money (p. 5)

2) $45.00 \div 12 = 3.75$; One baseball costs $3.75.

3) $44.25 \div 15 = 2.95 \rightarrow$ $2.95 per binder;
$2.95 \cdot 25 = 73.75 \rightarrow$ Henri spent $73.75 on binders.

4) Jeans: $24.95 \cdot 2 = 49.90$; shirts: $12.50 \cdot 3 = 37.50$;
$175.00 - 49.90 - 37.50 - 70.00 = 17.60 \rightarrow$
Brandon has $17.60 left.

5) Jorge earns x dollars; Juanita earns $2x$ dollars;
together they earn $x + 2x = 3x$ dollars.
$3x = 2,400 \rightarrow x = 2,400 \div 3 \rightarrow x = 800$
Jorge is paid $800.

6) Sales tax: $899.00 \cdot 0.06 = 53.94$;
$899.00 + 53.94 = 952.94$;
The total amount for the new sofa is $952.94.

7) Amount of discount: $12.95 \cdot 0.40 = 5.18$;
$12.95 - 5.18 = 7.77$; The sale price is $7.77.

8) $100.00 \div 16.99 \approx 5.89$; Five cartridges can be purchased.

The Mathematics of Lemonade Stands (p. 6–10)

1) $2.00 \div 5 = 0.40$; The cost per lemon is $0.40.

2) $2.25 \div 9 = 0.25$; Each cup of sugar costs $0.25.

3) To find the correct factor, I have to divide the amount I want by the amount the recipe makes.

$8 \div 1\frac{1}{2} = \frac{8}{1} \div \frac{3}{2} = \frac{8}{1} \cdot \frac{2}{3} = \frac{16}{3} = 5\frac{1}{3}$

To make 8 quarts of lemonade, I need to multiply the recipe by $5\frac{1}{3}$.

4) Lemons: $6 \cdot 5\frac{1}{3} = \dfrac{\overset{2}{\cancel{6}}}{1} \cdot \dfrac{16}{\underset{1}{\cancel{3}}} = \frac{32}{1} = 32$

Sugar: $\frac{3}{4} \cdot 5\frac{1}{3} = \dfrac{\overset{1}{\cancel{3}}}{\underset{1}{\cancel{4}}} \cdot \dfrac{\overset{4}{\cancel{16}}}{\underset{1}{\cancel{3}}} = \frac{4}{1} = 4$

I need 32 lemons and 4 cups of sugar to make 2 gallons of lemonade.

5) Lemons: $0.40 \cdot 32 = 12.80$
Sugar: $0.25 \cdot 4 = 1.00$
I need to spend $13.80 on lemons and sugar to make 2 gallons of lemonade.

6) $2 \cdot 128 = 256$; 256 ounces of lemonade in 2 gallons; $256 \div 8 = 32$; 32 cups sold
If I sell the entire 2 gallons of lemonade in 8-ounce cups, I will sell 32 cups.

7) $0.75 \cdot 32 = 24.00$; The income from selling 2 gallons of lemonade is $24.00.

8) The cost to make 2 gallons of lemonade is $13.80. The profit per day is $24.00 − $13.80 = $10.20. Running the stand for 2 days gives a total profit of $10.20 \cdot 2 = 20.40.

9) Answers will vary. Sample answer:
Since Alfonso and Bethany each work half the weekend, I can count them as one worker and divide their share in half. With Charlene and me, that makes three workers, so I can divide the profit by 3; $20.40 ÷ 3 = $6.80, so each worker earns $6.80. However, I have to divide that in half, giving Alfonso and Bethany each $6.80 ÷ 2 = $3.40. Charlene and I should each get $6.80 for the weekend.

10) Answers will vary. Sample answers:
1. Lemons are the most expensive part of the lemonade, so I could use one less lemon in the basic recipe, and therefore spend less. The problem that might arise is that the lemonade would not taste the same, and people may not like it as much, so they might not want to buy it.

2. I might consider having fewer people work at the lemonade stand, so I would have to split the profit among fewer workers. The problem could be not enough workers.

Unit 2: Dog Walking

Variable Expressions and Inequalities (p. 12)
2) $18 - s$
3) $23 + c$
4) $c - 16$
5) $p \geq 72$
6) $d < 345$
7) $s \leq 175$
8) $b > 500$

Least Common Multiple (p. 13)
2) Multiples of 4: 4, 8, 12, 16, 20, 24, 28, 32, 36; Multiples of 9: 9, 18, 27, 36; LCM (4, 9) = 36
3) Multiples of 10: 10, 20, 30, 40, 50, 60; Multiples of 12: 12, 24, 36, 48, 60; LCM (10, 12) = 60
4) Multiples of 3: 3, 6, 9, 12; Multiples of 12: 12, 24, 36; LCM (3, 12) = 12
5) Multiples of 2: 2, 4, 6, 8, 10, 12, 14, 16, 18, 20, 22, 24, 26, 28, 30; Multiples of 3: 3, 6, 9, 12, 15, 18, 21, 24, 27, 30; Multiples of 5: 5, 10, 15, 20, 25, 30; LCM (2, 3, 5) = 30
6) Multiples of 4: 4, 8, 12, 16, 20, 24; Multiples of 6: 6, 12, 18, 24; Multiples of 8: 8, 16, 24; LCM (4, 6, 8) = 24
7) Multiples of 2: 2, 4, 6, 8, 10, 12, 14, 16, 18, 20, 22, 24, 26, 28, 30, 32, 34, 36, 38, 40, 42, 44, 46, 48, 50, 52, 54, 56, 58, 60, 62, 64, 66, 68, 70; Multiples of 5: 5, 10, 15, 20, 25, 30, 35, 40, 45, 50, 55, 60, 65, 70; Multiples of 7: 7, 14, 21, 28, 35, 42, 49, 56, 63, 70; LCM (2, 5, 7) = 70
8) Multiples of 2: 2, 4, 6, 8, 10, 12, 14, 16, 18, 20, 22, 24, 26, 28, 30, 32, 34, 36; Multiples of 4: 4, 8, 12, 16, 20, 24, 28, 32, 36; Multiples of 6: 6, 12, 18, 24, 30, 36; Multiples of 9: 9, 18, 27, 36; LCM (2, 4, 6, 9) = 36

Statistical Quantities (p. 14)
2) Mean: 13; MAD: $1\frac{5}{11}$; Median: 13
3) Mean: 28; MAD: $4\frac{1}{3}$; Median: 27
4) Mean: 47; MAD: $8\frac{1}{4}$; Median: 46

The Mathematics of Dog Walking (p. 15–20)
1) Answers will vary.
2) Answers will vary.
3) Answers will vary but should be of the form $n - a$, where n represents the total number of hours calculated in Question 2.
4) $0 \leq a \leq 2$
(Since there cannot be negative hours spent)

5) The solutions to the given inequality can be any number that is less than or equal to 2. Since you cannot spend a negative amount of time, the number should also be greater than or equal to 0.

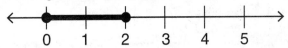

6)
a) Multiples of 6: 6, 12, 18, 24; Multiples of 8: 8, 16, 24; Multiples of 12: 12, 24; LCM (6, 8, 12) = 24; It will take 24 minutes. I used the listing method to determine the LCM.
b) Sample answer: I need to divide the LCM by the time it takes for each pair of dogs to walk one lap. Me: 24 ÷ 6 = 4 laps; Miranda: 24 ÷ 8 = 3 laps; D'Shaun: 24 ÷ 12 = 2 laps
7) Multiples of 3: 3, 6, 9, 12, 15, 18, 21, 24, 27, 30; Multiples of 2: 2, 4, 6, 8, 10, 12, 14, 16, 18, 20, 22, 24, 26, 28, 30; Multiples of 5: 5, 10, 15, 20, 25, 30; Multiples of 6: 6, 12, 18, 24, 30; LCM (2, 3, 5, 6) = 30. I used the listing method to determine the LCM, which shows that all four dogs will be walked on the same day again in 30 days.
8)
Time Spent on Administrative Tasks

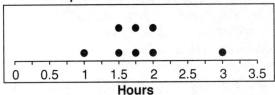

Hours

9) Sample answer: Most weeks I spend between 1.5 and 2 hours on administrative tasks.
10)
Time Spent Walking Dogs

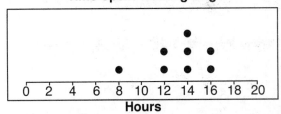

Hours

11) Sample answer: The most frequent amount of time spent walking dogs in a week is 14 hours.
12) Sample answer: On average, I spent $1\frac{13}{16}$ hours or about 1 hour and 49 minutes on administrative tasks each week.
13) Sample answer: On average, I spent $13\frac{1}{4}$ hours or about 13 hours and 15 minutes walking dogs each week.
14) Sample answer: On average, the time spent walking dogs each week varies from the mean by about 2 hours.
15)
a) Mean: $9\frac{3}{4}$; Median: 10

b) Sample answer: I will tell my friend the median because the mean and median are about the same, and the median is a whole number.

Unit 3: Fundraisers
Writing Ratios (p. 22)
Answers will vary. The following answers represent a sample of possible answers.

2) The ratio of green apples to red apples is 9:7. Out of 16 apples in Maurice's cart, 9 are green.
3) The ratio of Wii games to PS3 games is 8:6. For every 3 PS3 games Sarah has, she has 4 Wii games.
4) The ratio of black circles to gray circles is 1:1. The ratio of white circles to total circles is 4:12.
5) For every 7 girls in Ms. Holt's classroom, there are 5 boys. The ratio of girls to boys in Ms. Holt's classroom is 14:10.
6) Out of 30 ice cream cones sold, 12 were vanilla. The ratio of vanilla cones to chocolate cones is 2:3.
7) The ratio of red squares to blue triangles is 3:4. The ratio of blue triangles to total shapes is 4:7.
8) For every 25 bags of popcorn sold, 42 boxes of candy were sold. The ratio of bags of popcorn to boxes of candy sold is 125:210.

Division With Multi-Digit Numbers (p. 23)

2)
```
       484 r 1
   5 ) 2421
     - 20
       42
     - 40
       21
     - 20
        1
```

3)
```
         950
   91 ) 86450
      - 819
        455
      - 455
         00
```

4)
```
         489 r 13
   19 ) 9304
      - 76
        170
      - 152
        184
      - 171
         13
```

5)
```
        848
   4 ) 3392
     - 32
       19
     - 16
       32
     - 32
        0
```

6)
```
        288
   11 ) 3168
      - 22
        96
      - 88
        88
      - 88
         0
```

7)
```
         22.6
   72 ) 1627.2
      - 144
        187
      - 144
        432
      - 432
          0
```

8)
```
         277.8
   22 ) 6111.6
      - 44
        171
      - 154
        171
      - 154
        176
      - 176
          0
```

Unit Rates (p. 24)

2) Lucy read $270 \div 9$ or 30 pages each hour. It will take Lucy $390 \div 30$ or 13 hours to read 390 pages.
3) There are four 15-second periods in 1 minute. So Kaniah can type $10 \cdot 4$ or 40 words per minute.
4) $3.24 \div 9 = 0.36$
   The cost for one lemon is $0.36.
5) $27 \div 4.5 = 6$
   Mai earns $6 per hour.
6) There are two 30-minute periods in 1 hour. So Davon can hike $2.25 \cdot 2$ or 4.5 miles per hour. If he hikes for 7 hours, then David will hike $4.5 \cdot 7$ or 31.5 miles.
7) If it costs $37.50 for 15 gallons, then the unit cost is $37.50 \div 15$ or $2.50/gallon. Then, since $60 \div 2.50$ is 24, I can get 24 gallons of gas for $60.
8) I can run 6 miles in 1 hour and $6 \cdot 3$ is 18. So it will take me $1 \cdot 3$ or 3 hours to run 18 miles.

The Mathematics of Fundraisers (p. 25–29)

1) $(39.89 + 9.49) \cdot 18 = 888.84$
   The uniforms and hats will cost $888.84.

2) $349.20 + 4(65.49) = 611.16$
   They need $611.16 for equipment.

3) $888.84 + 611.16 = 1500.00$
   They need to raise $1,500 in all.

4)
a) Yes, this is a ratio that correctly represents the results. If you reduce 210:126, you get 5:3.
b) No, although the statement is correct, it does not use ratio reasoning.
c) Yes, this is a ratio that correctly represents the results. This compares the quantities using a part-to-whole comparison.

5) Answers will vary. The ratio of students choosing frozen pizzas to cookie dough is 84:252. The ratio of students choosing frozen pizzas to cookie dough is 1:3. Out of every 4 votes, 3 were for cookie dough.

6) $12x \geq 1,000$

   $\dfrac{12x}{12} \geq \dfrac{1,000}{12}$

   $x \geq 83.\overline{3}$

   They need to sell a minimum of 84 sweatshirts to earn at least $1,000.

7) $4.50x \geq 500$

   $\dfrac{4.50x}{4.50} \geq \dfrac{500}{4.50}$

   $x \geq 111.\overline{1}$

   They need to sell a minimum of 112 tubs of cookie dough to earn at least $500.

8) $\dfrac{4}{7} = \dfrac{16}{x}$

   To get a ratio equivalent to $\frac{4}{7}$, I need to multiply 7 by 4, which gives me 28. Pedro needs to ask 28 people to buy cookie dough to sell 16 tubs.

9) $\dfrac{3}{4} = \dfrac{9}{x}$

   To get a ratio equivalent to $\frac{3}{4}$, I need to multiply 4 by 3, which gives me 12. Dan needs to ask 12 people to sell 9 sweatshirts.

10) $107 \cdot 4.50 = 481.50$
    $115 \cdot 12 = 1,380$
    $1,380 + 481.50 = 1,861.50$
    The team earned $481.50 selling cookie dough and $1,380 selling sweatshirts. They raised $1861.50 total. Although they didn't sell $500 worth of cookie dough, they made up for it in sweatshirt sales. So yes, they met their fundraising goals.

Unit 4: Educators

Writing Equations (p. 31)

2) $b = 3a$
3) $n = 10m$
4) $q = 9p$
5) $t = s + 5$
6) $z = y + 10$
7) $x = w + 2$
8) $g = f + 7$

Area of Rectangles (p. 32)

2) $A = bh \Rightarrow A = (12\text{ cm})(9\text{ cm}) \Rightarrow A = 108\text{ cm}^2$;
   The area of the rectangle is 108 square centimeters.

3) $A = bh \Rightarrow A = (15\text{ ft})(17\text{ ft}) \Rightarrow A = 255\text{ ft}^2$;
   The area of the rectangle is 255 square feet.

4) $A = bh \Rightarrow A = (1.5\text{ m})(3.25\text{ m}) \Rightarrow A = 4.875\text{ m}^2$;
   The area of the rectangle is 4.875 square meters.

5) $A = bh \Rightarrow A = (1.24\text{ m})(0.41\text{ m}) \Rightarrow A = 0.5084\text{ m}^2$;
   The area of the rectangle is 0.5084 square meter.

6) $A = bh \Rightarrow A = (5.3\text{ yd})(5.3\text{ yd}) \Rightarrow A = 28.09\text{ yd}^2$;
   The area of the rectangle is 28.09 square yards.

7) $A = bh \Rightarrow A = (68\text{ cm})(113\text{ cm}) \Rightarrow A = 7,684\text{ cm}^2$;
   The area of the rectangle is 7,684 square centimeters.

8) $A = bh \Rightarrow A = (245\text{ mm})(137\text{ mm}) \Rightarrow A = 33,565\text{ mm}^2$; The area of the rectangle is 33,565 square millimeters.

Graphing Polygons (p. 33)

2) 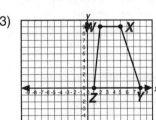   The figure is a rectangle.

3) 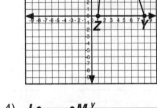   The figure is a trapezoid.

4) 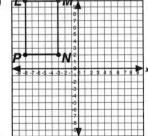   The figure is a rectangle.

5)

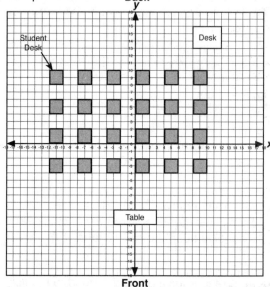

The figure is a trapezoid.

6)

The figure is a parallelogram.

The Mathematics of Educators (p. 34–38)

1)
a) The number of students represents the independent variable because it is independent of the number of folders.
b) The total number of folders represents the dependent variable because it is dependent on the number of students.
c) The total number of folders is the product of 5 and the number of students.
d) $f = 5s$

e)

Number of Students	Total Number of Folders
1	5
2	10
3	15
4	20
5	25
6	30

2)

Number of Students	Total Number of Pencils
1	4
2	8
3	12
4	16
5	20
6	24

3) Sample answer: Let *s* represent the number of students and *p* represent the number of pencils. Then the equation $p = 4s$ can be used to represent the relationship between the number of students and the total number of pencils.

4) $p = 4s \Rightarrow p = 4 \cdot 23 \Rightarrow p = 92$;
A total of 92 pencils are needed for 23 students.

5) If each box contains 30 pencils, then 3 boxes will contain 3 · 30 or 90 pencils. Therefore I will need 4 boxes to have enough pencils.

6)
a) $A = bh \Rightarrow A = (6\,\text{ft})(4\,\text{ft}) \Rightarrow A = 24\,\text{ft}^2$; I will need 24 square feet of material to cover the bulletin board.
b) Sample answer: The material is 3 feet wide. Each yard of material is 3 feet long. So I will need $2 \cdot 1\frac{1}{3}$ or $2\frac{2}{3}$ yards of material to cover the entire bulletin board.
c) I will not have any material left over, because $2\frac{2}{3}$ yards is equal to 8 feet of material. If the material is 3 feet wide, then $2\frac{2}{3}$ yards of material is 3 · 8 or 24 square feet.

7) Sample answer.

a) Sample answer: See diagram above. Coordinates of desk: (8, 16), (12, 16), (12, 13), (8, 13).
b) Sample answer: See diagram above. Coordinates of table: (−3, −9), (3, −9), (3, −11), (−3, −11).
c) Sample answer: The coordinates of the student desk are: (−12, 10), (−10, 10), (−10, 8), (−12, 8). Because the *y*-coordinates of the back corners of the desk are the same, I can calculate the difference of the *x*-coordinates to determine the length of the desk. So the length of the desk is −10 − −12 = −10 + 12 or 2. Similarly, because the *x*-coordinates of the side corners of the desk are the same, I can calculate the difference of their *y*-coordinates to determine the width of the desk. So the width of the desk is 10 − 8 or 2. Therefore the desk is 2 feet by 2 feet.
d) See diagram above.

Unit 5: Law Enforcement
Ratios and Proportions (p. 40)

2) $\frac{c}{28} = \frac{15}{44} \rightarrow 44c = 420 \div 44 \rightarrow c = \frac{420}{44} \rightarrow$
$c = \frac{105}{11} \rightarrow c = 9\frac{6}{11}$

3) Female drivers: $140 - 112 = 28$; $28:112 = 1:4$

4) $\frac{18}{a} = \frac{5}{14} \rightarrow 252 = 5a \rightarrow a = 252 \div 5 \rightarrow$
$a = \frac{252}{5} \rightarrow a = 50.4$

5) $\frac{11}{6} = \frac{n}{10} \rightarrow 110 = 6n \rightarrow n = 110 \div 6 \rightarrow$
$n = \frac{110}{6} \rightarrow n = \frac{55}{3} \rightarrow n = 18\frac{1}{3}$

6) $\frac{750}{1} = \frac{16,500}{x} \rightarrow 750x = 16,500 \rightarrow$

$x = 16,500 \div 750 \rightarrow x = 22$; 22 police officers

7) $\frac{8}{5} = \frac{72}{x} \rightarrow 8x = 360 \rightarrow x = 360 \div 8 \rightarrow x = 45$;
45 pairs of pants

8) $\frac{8}{15} = \frac{7}{x} \rightarrow 8x = 105 \rightarrow x = \frac{105}{8} \rightarrow x = 13\frac{1}{8}$ or
13.125

Statistical Quantities (p. 41)

2) The only value that occurs more than once is 19, so the mode is 19.

3) Range = high − low; range = $22 - 10 = 12$

4) Median is the middle value; median = 18

5) First quartile (Q1) is the middle of the lower half of the data.;
$Q1 = \frac{13 + 14}{2} = \frac{27}{2} = 13\frac{1}{2}$

6) Third quartile (Q3) is the middle of the upper half of the data.;
$Q3 = \frac{19 + 21}{2} = \frac{40}{2} = 20$

7) IQR = Q3 − Q1 = $20 - 13\frac{1}{2} = 6\frac{1}{2}$

8) Mean absolute deviation is the average distance of each data point from the mean.; $3\frac{1}{9}$

Percents (p. 42)

2) $\frac{35}{100} = \frac{98}{x} \rightarrow 35x = 9,800 \rightarrow 9,800 \div 35 \rightarrow$
$x = 280$

3) $\frac{x}{100} = \frac{76}{32} \rightarrow 32x = 7,600 \rightarrow x = 7,600 \div 32 \rightarrow$
$x = 237.5\%$

4) $\frac{216}{100} = \frac{x}{153} \rightarrow 33,048 = 100x \rightarrow x = 33,048 \div 100 \rightarrow$
$x = 330.48$

5) 16 total values; 11 odd values; $\frac{11}{16} = 0.6875 = 68.75\%$;
68.75% of the values are odd

6) Sales tax: $2,249 \cdot 0.06 = 134.94$;
$2,249.00 + 134.94 = 2,383.94$;
total paid is $2,383.94

7) 2 boys + 3 girls = 5 students; $\frac{3}{5} = 0.6 = 60\%$;
60% of the students are girls

8) Amount of discount: $42.50 \cdot 0.30 = 12.75$;
$42.50 - 12.75 = 29.75$; sale price is $29.75

The Mathematics of Law Enforcement (p. 43–47)

1)
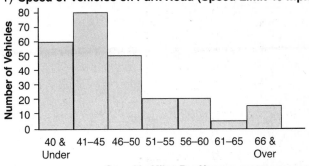
Speed of Vehicles on Park Road (Speed Limit 40 mph)

2) Number of drivers traveling from 41 to 50 mph:
$80 + 50 = 130$
Total number of drivers:
$60 + 80 + 50 + 20 + 20 + 5 + 15 = 250$;
$\frac{130}{250} = 0.52 = 52\%$; 52% of drivers travel up to 10 mph above the posted speed limit.

3) Number of drivers traveling 66 mph or over: 15
$\frac{15}{250} = 0.06 = 6\%$; 6% of drivers travel 66 mph or over.

$\frac{6}{100} = \frac{x}{1000} \rightarrow 6,000 = 100x \rightarrow x = 6,000 \div 100$
$\rightarrow x = 60$; Out of 1,000 drivers, 60 are expected to be reckless.

4) $100(80 + 50) + 175(20 + 20 + 5) + 350(15) =$
$100(130) + 175(45) + 350(15) =$
$13,000 + 7,875 + 5,250 = 26,125$
$26,125.00 in fines would be collected if each person speeding were ticketed.

5)
a)
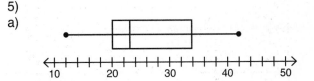

b) $12 + 17 + 19 + 20 + 21 + 21 + 21 + 25 +$
$28 + 31 + 34 + 35 + 38 + 42 = 364$;
$364 \div 14 = 26$;
Each student rode for about 26 hours.

6) Total schools visited: $5 \cdot 6 = 30$;
$\frac{30}{96} = 0.3125 = 31.25\%$
Officer Hernandez will visit 31.25% of schools in the region.

7) Total area: $85 \cdot 147 = 12,495$ square feet
$\frac{1}{300} = \frac{x}{12495} \rightarrow 12,495 = 300x \rightarrow$
$x = 12,495 \div 300 \rightarrow x = 41.65$
You must round up to ensure adequate coverage, so 42 security officers are needed.

8) $\frac{3}{100} = \frac{x}{1240} \rightarrow 3,720 = 100x \rightarrow$
$x = 3,720 \div 100 \rightarrow x = 37.2$
You must round up to ensure adequate coverage, so 38 security officers are needed.

9) Overtime rate: $1.5 \cdot 28.34 = 42.51$;
Total pay: $42.51 \cdot 7 = 297.57$
Officer Hernandez gets paid $297.57 for her shift as a security officer.

Unit 6: Bankers

Integers in the Real World (p. 49)
2) 9,650
3) −5
4) −585
5) 83
6) −12
7) 98
8) −15
9) −1,700
10) −14

Which One is Greater? (p. 50)
2) Jerome's first running play has the greater value.
$6 > -8$
3) The temperature in February has the greater value.
$-12 > -15$
4) Finding $3 is greater than losing $12. $3 > -12$
5) The boiling point of water is greater than the boiling point of chloroform. $0 > -63.5$
6) The scuba diver has greater location. $-25 > -800$
7) Damon's score has a greater value than Jeff's score.
$-1 > -3$; However, in golf the lower score wins, so Jeff is actually the winner.
8) Saundra's account is greater than Lina's.
$233 > -238$

Percent Problems (p. 51)
2) $\frac{8}{20} = \frac{x}{100} \rightarrow \frac{8}{20} = \frac{40}{100}$; 8 is 40% of 20.
3) $\frac{x}{45} = \frac{20}{100} \rightarrow \frac{x}{45} = \frac{1}{5} \rightarrow \frac{9}{45} = \frac{1}{5} \rightarrow x = 9$;
9 is 20% of 45.
4) $\frac{18}{x} = \frac{75}{100} \rightarrow \frac{18}{x} = \frac{3}{4} \rightarrow \frac{18}{24} = \frac{3}{4} \rightarrow x = 24$;
18 is 75% of 24.
5) $\frac{15}{100} = \frac{x}{200} \rightarrow \frac{15}{100} = \frac{30}{200} \rightarrow x = 30$;
15% of 200 is 30.
6) $\frac{14}{56} = \frac{x}{100} \rightarrow \frac{1}{4} = \frac{x}{100} \rightarrow \frac{1}{4} = \frac{25}{100} \rightarrow x = 25$;
14 is 25% of 56.
7) $\frac{75}{100} = \frac{x}{120} \rightarrow \frac{3}{4} = \frac{x}{120} \rightarrow \frac{3}{4} = \frac{90}{120} \rightarrow x = 90$;
75% of 120 is 90.
8) $\frac{15}{300} = \frac{x}{100} \rightarrow \frac{15}{300} = \frac{5}{100} \rightarrow x = 5$;
15 is 5% of 300.

The Mathematics of Bankers (p. 52–56)
1)
a) Ms. Moiamedi's balance is closer to zero; $-35 < 15$
b) Ms. Abdous' balance is closer to zero; $-598 < -375$

c) Mr. Augustine's and Ms. Mauger's balances are the same distance from zero; $145 > -145$
d) Mr. Lundell's balance is closer to zero; $415 < 475$
e) Ms. Mauger's balance is closer to zero; $-145 > -375$
2) Ms. Wohl has the largest balance.
3) Mr. Kozlova has the largest debt.
4) I can compare balances by thinking about how far they are from zero. Balances that are positive are greater than balances that are negative. I can compare two positive balances by determining which one is farther from zero; that one is the greater. I can compare two negative balances the same way, but the one that is closer to zero is greater.

5)

Bank Activity	Integer Representation
Deposit of $450	450
Debit of $135	−135
Credit of $99	99
Withdrawal of $75	−75
Deposit of $3,525	3,525
Credit of $429	429
Withdrawal of $1,050	−1,050
Debit of $750	−750

6)

Entry		Correct? (Y/N)	Corrected Value
Debit of $55	55	N	−55
Credit of $469	469	Y	
Credit of $947.25	−947.25	N	947.25
Debit of $64.75	64.75	N	−64.75
Debit of $777	−777	Y	
Credit of $129.50	−129.50	N	129.50
Credit of $57.50	57.50	Y	

7) The numbers are the same distance from zero, but they're on opposite sides of 0.
8) $\frac{5}{100} = \frac{x}{350,000}$
$\frac{5}{100} = \frac{3,500(5)}{3,500(100)} = \frac{17,500}{350,000}$
$x = 17,500$; Her commission is $17,500.

9) $\dfrac{52,500}{1,500,000} = \dfrac{x}{100}$

$\dfrac{105}{3,000} = \dfrac{x}{100}$

$\dfrac{21}{600} = \dfrac{x}{100}$

$\dfrac{7}{200} = \dfrac{x}{100}$

$x = 3.5$; 3.5% commission was earned by this sale.

10) $\dfrac{12}{100} = \dfrac{x}{7,500}$

$\dfrac{12}{100} = \dfrac{75(12)}{75(100)} = \dfrac{900}{7,500}$

$x = 900$; The bank is charging her \$900 in interest.

11) $\dfrac{1,125}{12,000} = \dfrac{x}{100}$

$1,125(100) = 12,000x$

$\dfrac{112,500}{12,000} = \dfrac{12,000x}{12,000}$

$x = 9.375$; The percent interest is 9.375%

Unit 7: Veterinarians

Writing Equations (p. 58)

2) Let g represent gallons and q represent quarts. Then $q = 4g$.

3) Let c represent centimeters and m represent millimeters. Then $m = 10c$.

4) Let p represent pounds and z represent ounces. Then $z = 16p$.

5) Let n represent inches and c represent centimeters. Then $c = 2.54n$.

6) Let e represent Euros and d represent U.S. dollars. Then $d = 1.127e$.

7) Let l represent liters and g represent gallons. Then $g = 0.264l$.

8) Let e represent pounds on Earth and m represent pounds on the moon. Then $m = 0.17e$.

Statistical Questions (p. 59)

2) This is *not* a good statistical question because it does not allow for variability.

3) This is a good statistical question because it allows for variability. The attribute being measured is how much students like school. It is measured on a scale of 1 to 10.

4) This is a good statistical question because it allows for variability. The attribute being measured is the number of years my teammates have played soccer. It is measured in years.

5) This is *not* a good statistical question because it does not allow for variability.

6) This is a good statistical question because it allows for variability. The attribute being measured is the age of teachers in my school. It is being measured in years.

Graphing Data Sets (p. 60)

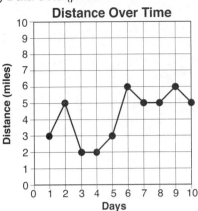
Distance Over Time

The Mathematics of Veterinarians (p. 61–65)

1)
a) $12 \text{ kg} \cdot \dfrac{2.2 \text{ lb}}{1 \text{ kg}} = 26.4 \text{ lb}$;

Jack weighs 26.4 pounds.

b) Let p represent pounds and k represent kilograms. Then $p = 2.2k$.

2)
a) Jack's owner should give him 5 • 26.4 or 132 milligrams of amoxicillin every 12 hours.

b) I will need to give Jack's owner 2 • 132 • 10 or 2,640 milligrams of amoxicillin. Because Jack must take 132 milligrams every 12 hours, he will need 2 doses a day. So I multiplied 132 by 2. Then he must take the amoxicillin for 10 days. So I multiplied the result by 10.

3)
a) $p = 2.2k = 2.2 \cdot 7.5 = 16.5$; Cleo weighs 16.5 pounds.

b) I will need to give Cleo's owner 4 • 165 • 8 or 5,280 milligrams of tetracycline. Because Cleo must take 10 milligrams per pound every 6 hours, she will need 4 doses of 10 • 16.5 or 165 milligrams a day. So I multiplied 165 by 4. Then she must take the tetracycline for 8 days. So I multiplied the result by 8.

4) Sample graph:

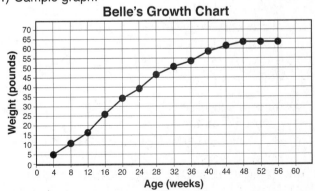
Belle's Growth Chart

5) Sample answer: Belle grew very rapidly in the first 36 weeks, but her growth slowed and leveled off after that.

6)

a) Belle grows 6 pounds in 4 weeks. So her unit growth rate is 1.5 pounds per week.

b) Sample answer: It means that Belle would grow 1.5 pounds every week. So at 5 weeks, she would weigh 6.5 pounds and so on.

c)

Age (weeks)	Weight (pounds)	Age (weeks)	Weight (pounds)
4	5	13	18.5
5	6.5	14	20
6	8	15	21.5
7	9.5	16	23
8	11	17	24.5
9	12.5	18	26
10	14	19	27.5
11	15.5	20	29
12	17		

d) Sample graph:

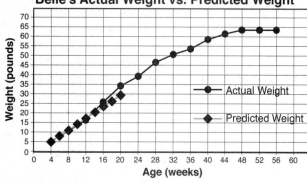

Belle's Actual Weight vs. Predicted Weight

e) Sample answer: Let w represent Belle's age in weeks since week 4 (or current week minus 4) and p represent Belle's weight in pounds. Then $p = 1.5w + 5$. The $+ 5$ refers to Belle's weight at week 4.

f) $p = 1.5w + 5 \Rightarrow p = 1.5(56 - 4) + 5 \Rightarrow$
$p = 1.5(52) + 5 \Rightarrow p = 78 + 5 \Rightarrow p = 83$;
Sample answer: This answer is not reasonable, because Belle weighed 63 pounds at 56 weeks. Further, it is not reasonable to think that a dog will continue to grow at a constant rate throughout his or her life.

7)

a) Sample answer. They are all pretty good statistical questions, as they allow for variability in the data. Question 2 would be better if a rating scale was provided.

b) Answers will vary.

Unit 8: Computer Programming

Operations With Rational Numbers (p. 67)

2) $\frac{3}{4} - \frac{5}{6} = \frac{9}{12} - \frac{10}{12} = -\frac{1}{12}$

3) $3^7 = 2{,}187$

4) $\left(-1\frac{2}{5}\right) - \left(-6\frac{2}{3}\right) = -\frac{7}{5} - \left(-\frac{20}{3}\right) = -\frac{7}{5} + \frac{20}{3} =$
$-\frac{21}{15} + \frac{100}{15} = \frac{79}{15}$ or $5\frac{4}{15}$

5) $6\frac{7}{8} \div \frac{5}{16} = \frac{55}{8} \div \frac{5}{16} = \frac{\overset{11}{\cancel{55}}}{\cancel{8}} \cdot \frac{\overset{2}{\cancel{16}}}{\cancel{5}} = \frac{22}{1} = 22$

6) $22\frac{7}{10} + \left(-11\frac{1}{2}\right) = \frac{227}{10} + \left(-\frac{23}{2}\right) = \frac{227}{10} - \frac{23}{2} =$
$\frac{227}{10} - \frac{115}{10} = \frac{112}{10} = \frac{56}{5}$ or $11\frac{1}{5}$

7) $5\frac{1}{4} - \left(-3\frac{7}{8}\right) = \frac{21}{4} - \left(-\frac{31}{8}\right) = \frac{21}{4} + \frac{31}{8} = \frac{42}{8} + \frac{31}{8}$
$= \frac{73}{8}$ or $9\frac{1}{8}$

8) $\left(\frac{2}{5}\right)^4 = \frac{2^4}{5^4} = \frac{16}{625}$

Algebraic Equations (p. 68)

2) $m = 30t$

3) $4y = 30 \Rightarrow \frac{\cancel{4}y}{\cancel{4}} = \frac{30}{4} \Rightarrow y = \frac{15}{2}$ or $y = 7\frac{1}{2}$

4) $n + 5\frac{1}{4} = 12\frac{2}{3} \Rightarrow n + \cancel{5\frac{1}{4}} - \cancel{5\frac{1}{4}} = 12\frac{2}{3} - 5\frac{1}{4} \Rightarrow$
$n = 12\frac{8}{12} - 5\frac{3}{12} \Rightarrow n = 7\frac{5}{12}$

5) $\frac{4}{9}b = 2\frac{3}{5} \Rightarrow \frac{\cancel{9}}{\cancel{4}} \cdot \frac{\cancel{4}}{\cancel{9}}b = 2\frac{3}{5} \cdot \frac{9}{4} \Rightarrow b = \frac{13}{5} \cdot \frac{9}{4} \Rightarrow$
$b = \frac{117}{20}$ or $b = 5\frac{17}{20}$

6) $t = h + 3\frac{1}{2}$

7) $x + \frac{3}{10} = \frac{1}{4} \Rightarrow x + \cancel{\frac{3}{10}} - \cancel{\frac{3}{10}} = \frac{1}{4} - \frac{3}{10} \Rightarrow$
$x = \frac{5}{20} - \frac{6}{20} \Rightarrow x = -\frac{1}{20}$

8) $\frac{5}{7}p = 70 \Rightarrow \frac{\cancel{7}}{\cancel{5}} \cdot \frac{\cancel{5}}{\cancel{7}}p = 70 \cdot \frac{7}{5} \Rightarrow p = \frac{\overset{14}{\cancel{70}}}{1} \cdot \frac{7}{\cancel{5}} \Rightarrow$
$p = \frac{98}{1} \Rightarrow p = 98$

Geometric Calculations (p. 69)

2) $V = s^3 = \left(\frac{3}{4}\right)^3 = \frac{3^3}{4^3} = \frac{27}{64}$;

The volume of the cube is $\frac{27}{64}$ in.³.

3) $|7 - (-4)| = |7 + 4| = |11| = 11$;
The distance between the points is 11 units.

4)

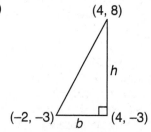

Base: $b = |4 - (-2)| = |4 + 2| = |6| = 6$;
Height: $h = |8 - (-3)| = |8 + 3| = |11| = 11$

Area: $A = \frac{1}{2}bh = \frac{1}{2} \cdot 6 \cdot 11 = \frac{1}{\cancel{2}} \cdot \frac{\overset{3}{\cancel{6}}}{1} \cdot \frac{11}{1} = \frac{33}{1} = 33$;
The triangle has an area of 33 units².

5)

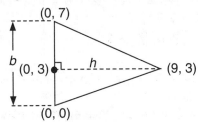

Base: $b = |7 - 0| = |7| = 7$;
Height: $h = |9 - 0| = |9| = 9$;
Area: $A = \frac{1}{2}bh = \frac{1}{2} \cdot 7 \cdot 9 = \frac{1}{2} \cdot \frac{7}{1} \cdot \frac{9}{1} =$
$\frac{63}{2}$ or $31\frac{1}{2}$; The triangle has an area of $31\frac{1}{2}$ units².

6) $V = lwh = 2 \cdot 1\frac{1}{4} \cdot \frac{2}{3} = \frac{\cancel{2}}{1} \cdot \frac{5}{\underset{\cancel{2}\,1}{\cancel{4}}} \cdot \frac{\cancel{2}}{3} = \frac{5}{3}$ or $1\frac{2}{3}$;

The volume of the box is $1\frac{2}{3}$ ft.³.

7) $|-3 - (-18)| = |-3 + 18| = |15| = 15$; The distance between the points is 15 units.

8) $A = lw = \frac{7}{8} \cdot 6\frac{2}{5} = \frac{7}{\cancel{8}} \cdot \frac{\overset{4}{\cancel{32}}}{5} = \frac{28}{5}$ or $5\frac{3}{5}$;

The area of the rectangle is $5\frac{3}{5}$ m².

The Mathematics of Computer Programming (p. 70–74)
1)
a) The screen is cut in half both horizontally and vertically.
Horizontal: $1{,}920 \div 2 = 960$;
Vertical: $1{,}200 \div 2 = 600$
The corners are located at $(-960, -600)$, $(-960, 600)$, $(960, 600)$, and $(960, -600)$.
b) Moving up changes the y-coordinate. The equation is $y = -286 + 28t$.
c) Moving right changes the x-coordinate. The equation is $x = -325 + 42t$.
d) The first object would have to move up the screen until its y-coordinate becomes the same as the second object's y-coordinate. Likewise, the second object would have to move right until its x-coordinate becomes the same as the first object's x-coordinate. Both actions would have to take the same amount of time.
First object: $190 = -286 + 28t \Rightarrow$
$190 + 286 = 28t \Rightarrow 28t = 476 \Rightarrow t = 17$
Second object: $389 = -325 + 42t \Rightarrow$
$389 + 325 = 42t \Rightarrow 42t = 714 \Rightarrow t = 17$
The two objects will collide 17 seconds after they start moving.

2)
a) $V = lwh = 4\frac{1}{2} \cdot 3 \cdot 1\frac{1}{2} = \frac{9}{2} \cdot \frac{3}{1} \cdot \frac{3}{2} = \frac{81}{4}$ or $20\frac{1}{4}$
An effective wall is at least $20\frac{1}{4}$ units³.
b) Each cube: $V = s^3 = \left(\frac{1}{2}\right)^3 = \frac{1^3}{2^3} = \frac{1}{8}$;

Number of cubes: $20\frac{1}{4} \div \frac{1}{8} = \frac{81}{\cancel{4}} \cdot \frac{\overset{2}{\cancel{8}}}{1} = \frac{162}{1} = 162$

There must be 162 building blocks available to construct an effective wall.
c) Total cost of wall: $162 \cdot 3 = 486$ tokens; number of puzzles solved: $486 \div 20 = 24.3$; Since at least 486 tokens are needed, 25 puzzles must be solved to purchase the blocks.

3)
a) The number of villains is multiplied by 2 each time a new player joins the game, so the total number of villains is 2 multiplied by 2 another 5 times, which gives $2^6 = 64$. There will be 64 villains after the fifth new player joins the game.
b) Rafael is located at $(0, 0)$. Naoki is located at $(0, -28)$. The location of the farthest point directly ahead of Rafael that is shown on the screen is $(0, 75)$. The distance between Naoki and that point is
$|75 - (-28)| = |75 + 28| = |103| = 103$ ft.
Therefore, Sergei's character can be at most 103 ft ahead of Naoki's character while still being displayed on Rafael's computer screen.
c) Naoki's character can be located at either $(-23, 0)$ or $(0, -45)$, represented by point N in each of the following right triangles:

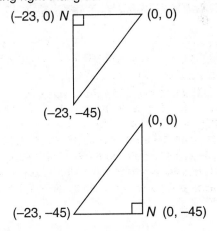

Unit 9: Air Traffic Controllers
Distance, Rate, and Time Problems (p. 76)
2) $d = rt \Rightarrow d = 8.5(3) \Rightarrow d = 25.5$
The distance is 25.5 miles.

3) $d = rt \Rightarrow d = 14\left(\frac{3}{4}\right) \Rightarrow d = 10\frac{1}{2}$
The distance is $10\frac{1}{2}$ miles.

4) $d = rt \rightarrow 12 = 8t \rightarrow 12 \div 8 = 8t \div 8 \rightarrow$
1.5 = t; It will take 1.5 hours.

5) $d = rt \rightarrow d = 780(3) \rightarrow d = 2,340$
The airplane can travel 2,340 miles.

6) $d = rt \rightarrow 15 = 1.5r \rightarrow 15 \div 1.5 = 1.5r \div 1.5$
$\rightarrow 10 = r$; Nora rides her bike 10 mph.

7) $d = rt \rightarrow 9 = 1.25r \rightarrow 9 \div 1.25 = 1.25r \div 1.25$
$\rightarrow 7.2 = r$; Juan roller skates 7.2 mph.

8) $d = rt \rightarrow 51 = 34t \rightarrow 51 \div 34 = 34t \div 34 \rightarrow$
1.5 = r; The train will take 1.5 hours to travel 51 miles.

Algebraic Equations (p. 77)

2) $45 + x = 63 \rightarrow 45 - 45 + x = 63 - 45 \rightarrow$
$x = 18$; 18 likes were added.

3) $x + 30 = 47 \rightarrow x + 30 - 30 = 47 - 30 \rightarrow$
$x = 17$; Anthony ran 17 miles.

4) $x + 17 = 29.5 \rightarrow x + 17 - 17 = 29.5 - 17 \rightarrow$
$x = 12.5$; The number is 12.5.

5) $x + 20 = 38 \rightarrow x + 20 - 20 = 38 - 20 \rightarrow$
$x = 18$; \$18 was originally in his wallet.

6) $35 + x = 48 \rightarrow 35 - 35 + x = 48 - 35 \rightarrow$
$x = 13$; She increased her speed by 13 mph.

7) $68 + x = 115 \rightarrow 68 - 68 + x = 115 - 68 \rightarrow$
$x = 47$; The number is 47.

8) $x + 785 = 993 \rightarrow x + 785 - 785 = 993 - 785$
$\rightarrow x = 208$; The number is 208.

9) $515 + x = 900 \rightarrow 515 - 515 + x = 900 - 515$
$\rightarrow x = 385$; The number is 385.

10) $225 + x = 400 \rightarrow 225 - 225 + x = 400 - 225$
$\rightarrow x = 175$; The temperature needs to increase by 175°F.

Substitute to Verify Equations (p. 78)

2) $15 - 6x = 9 \rightarrow 15 - 6(1) = 9 \rightarrow 15 - 6 = 9$
$\rightarrow 9 = 9$; Yes, the equation is true for this value of x.

3) $\frac{8 + 2}{8 - 3} = 2 \rightarrow \frac{10}{5} = 2 \rightarrow 2 = 2$

Yes, the equation is true for this value of x.

4) $4(2) - 4 = 0 \rightarrow 8 - 4 = 0 \rightarrow 4 = 0$
No, the equation is not true for this value of x.

5) $\frac{19 - 5}{2} = \frac{19 + 2}{3} \rightarrow \frac{14}{2} = \frac{21}{3} \rightarrow 7 = 7$

Yes, the equation is true for this value of x.

6) $4(3) - 6 = 6 \rightarrow 12 - 6 = 6 \rightarrow 6 = 6$
Yes, the equation is true for this value of x.

7) $\frac{5(3)}{2} = 3(3) + 5 \rightarrow \frac{15}{2} = 9 + 5 \rightarrow 7.5 = 14$

No, the equation is not true for this value of x.

8) $2[3(4) - 4] = 3(4) + 1 \rightarrow 2(12 - 4) = 12 + 1$
$\rightarrow 2(8) = 13 \rightarrow 16 = 13$
No, the equation is not true for this value of x.

The Mathematics of Air Traffic Controllers (p. 79–83)

1)
a) $126 = 420t$
b) $145 = 435t$
c) UA2439: $126 = 420t \rightarrow 126 \div 420 = 420t \div 420$
$\rightarrow 0.3 = t$
WS745: $145 = 435t \rightarrow 145 \div 435 = 435t \div 435$
$\rightarrow 0.(\overline{33}) = t$
Flight UA2439 will arrive first in 0.3 hour, or 18 minutes. WS745 will arrive in $0.(\overline{33})$ hour or 20 minutes.
d) $145 = 360t \rightarrow 145 \div 360 = 360t \div 360 \rightarrow$
$0.403 = t$; It will now take approximately 0.403 hour or 24 minutes.

2) $d = 145(0.25) \rightarrow d = 36.25$
The final approach will cover 36.25 miles.

3) $34,550 + x = 38,452 \rightarrow$
$34,550 - 34,550 + x = 38,452 - 34,550 \rightarrow$
$x = 3,902$
The pilot should ascend 3,902 feet.

4) $560 = 250t \rightarrow 560 \div 250 = 250t \div 250 \rightarrow$
$2.24 = t$; It will take 2.24 hours or about 2 hours and 14 minutes.

5)
a) $6,500 + x = 11,500 \rightarrow$
$6,500 - 6,500 + x = 11,500 - 6,500 \rightarrow x = 5,000$
The aircraft increases 5,000 feet in altitude.
b) $250 + x = 400 \rightarrow 250 - 250 + x = 400 - 250$
$\rightarrow x = 150$; The speed increases 150 mph.
c) $530 = 400t \rightarrow 530 \div 400 = 400t \div 400 \rightarrow$
$1.325 = t$; It will now take 1.325 hours or about 1 hour and 20 minutes.

6) $d = rt \rightarrow 1,995 = (570)(3) \rightarrow 1,995 = 1,710$
This is not a good plan. The distance of 1,995 miles is not equal to the rate of 570 mph times the 3-hour time.

7) $d = rt \rightarrow 1,995 = (665)(3) \rightarrow 1,995 = 1,995$
Yes, this plan will work. The distance of 1,995 equals the rate of 665 mph times the 3-hour time.

8) The least common multiple of 6 and 8 is 24. In 24 minutes, the tower controller will have 2 planes pushing back at the same time.

9) The least common multiple of 9 and 10 is 90. In 90 minutes, the tower controller will have 2 planes pushing back at the same time.